ARSÈNE LUPIN
PUZZLES

ARSÈNE LUPIN

PUZZLES

Adventures
and Mysteries
Inspired by the
Gentleman Thief

Joel Jessup

This edition published in 2023 by Arcturus Publishing Limited
26/27 Bickels Yard, 151–153 Bermondsey Street,
London SE1 3HA

AD010625NT

Printed in the UK

Contents

Introduction

ARSÈNE LUPIN IS NOT the king of thieves, for he desires not to rule over anyone. Rather, he is the thief of kings: a stealer of immeasurably valuable items, but with an integrity that would see him knock the undeserving from their pedestal with the lightest kick from a polished shoe. No story you hear of Lupin is implausible, and only a few are impossible. Criminals have on occasion had cause to impersonate police officers: Lupin was the head of the Sûreté for four years! His mastery of disguise is so complete that even he barely recognizes himself in the mirror.

Maurice Leblanc began documenting Lupin's adventures in 1905, claiming a friendship and a kind of informal agreement with the master thief that he would become his documentarian. You can still read his excellent short narratives in collections such as *Arsène Lupin, Gentleman Thief* and *Arsene Lupin vs. Herlock Sholmes*, and his longer novels such as *The Hollow Needle* and *813*. These tales have led to countless adaptations in film, television and other mediums, further expanding the mythology of Lupin. But despite Leblanc's 39 short stories and 17 novels, there remain yet more stories of Lupin's life and encounters that had been untold, and I collect them here for your consideration. Each of the stories contains a puzzle of sorts, whether a mystery to solve, a mathematical conundrum to calculate or a twist of logic to unravel. The tales come from first-hand accounts scribbled down in long-lost diaries, hastily redacted police reports and oral histories passed down through generations, and some of them may even have been laid down by Lupin himself! There may be contradictions of history or happenstance in their telling, but the legend of Lupin is so infused with trickery and subterfuge that it's inevitable some things have got tangled up. Some of the characters in this book never appeared in Leblanc's original telling, but it cannot be certain if Lupin never told Leblanc about them, or if it was agreed they would be excised from the record.

As you read these puzzles, remember: sometimes Lupin is the instigator of their mystery, and sometimes the investigator. Sometimes you will not know who Lupin is in the tale, and sometimes it is he who tells the tale to you. To paraphrase Lupin himself, he cares not if you know exactly who he is or what he looks like: He only cares that you know what he has done!

Puzzles

The Sunset Ruby

A S YOU ENTER THE fabled treasure room at the palace of Versailles, the police commissary steps forward.

"We must move swiftly! The Sunset Ruby has been stolen from its case in the middle of the room! Arsène Lupin sent a message saying he would take it, and he has! But we are lucky! He did not anticipate the new security arrangements, and these mechanical shutters have blocked all escape! This means one of the people in this room must be Lupin! And we must find out who."

You cast your eyes over the room's other occupants as further police agents filter in behind you. An aged woman, faint from the shock. A man dressed as Pantaloon the clown, miming annoyance. A dashing young soldier with an eyepatch. And a small man in a smart suit.

The commissary is baffled, rubbing his chalky white neck. "Surely none of these people can be Lupin! He is handsome, average height and weight, age roughly between 30–40. But he is a master of disguise . . ."

The police swiftly but delicately search all inside for the ruby. The small man lifts his trousers, showing his short legs with displeasure. "First that man in an overcoat pushes me out of the way, now this!"

The young soldier lifts his eyepatch to show that his empty eye socket does not conceal the ruby. A policeman gently touches the aged woman's face and confirms her many wrinkles are not a mask.

Another overenthusiastic young policeman attempts to pull Pantaloon's fake hooked nose off to see if the ruby is underneath, only to learn it is a real hooked nose, tripping over a discarded overcoat and falling onto the large sculpture in the room's corner! Pantaloon clutches his now reddened nose, further smearing his poorly applied makeup. "I came here to entertain les enfants, not be assaulted!"

Q: Which person in the room is Arsène Lupin?

The Stained Glass Windows

"I HEARD A TALE OF Arsène Lupin . . ." said the mustachioed man in the seat opposite me at the dinner party (and I leaned forward, because of course now I immediately assumed *he* was Lupin . . .).

"I heard a tale of Arsène Lupin gaining access to the count's upper chambers through employment of a window cleaner's scaffold suspended on the outside of the building. He knew the count was vain about his beautiful stained glass windows. However he faced a challenge, as the scaffold was carefully balanced, and the room's contents were heavy, so the items he took had to balance equally on the left and right side of him, or it would overbalance and spill the contents to the ground!"

Grabbing a napkin, he began writing down the respective items, but found himself unable to remember their exact weights.

"I remember the Rodin bronze was 26 kg . . . There was a beautiful Sormani Ormolu-mounted side table that was about 3 kg less . . . the heaviest thing was this Roman statue of Venus that they thought was from Pompeii, that was double the weight of the table plus one. Oh, this solid gold tureen, an ugly thing but easily fenced once melted down; if you doubled its weight then took away 10 kg, you would have the bronze's weight. And finally a commode in green velvet, would you believe, 2 kg less than the tureen."

My head swam as I tried to follow all the numbers.

Q: What are the weights of the items, and how should they be arranged on the left and right of Lupin to balance the scaffold?

The Society of Blanc et Noir

ARSÈNE LUPIN ONCE HAD cause to infiltrate the Society of Blanc et Noir. An elite club, the society considered themselves powerful but were more interested in having decadent balls behind closed doors where all the participants had to dress a very particular way, only black or white, sharply pressed clothes without a hint of stain, matching gloves for the men and matching earrings for the women. Lupin naturally brought matched pairs of black and white gloves with him in case of having to change his outfit suddenly.

After circulating the room, feigning interest at months-old gossip and intrigue, Lupin stole through to a small pitch-black ante room where his real prize lay: the money press! The society's members thrived not through their own work but from their ability to print a river of forged francs!

Lupin carefully removed the plate of the printing press that held the franc's design, but in the process he got ink all over his hands!

Outside he heard voices inquiring after his disappearance. He needed to cover his ink-stained hands before he returned to the party. But in the effort of removing the plate, his collection of spare gloves had become mixed in their pouch, some white, some black, with no indication of which!

Lupin had but a few seconds to pull gloves from the pouch, which he could then pull on as he left the room!

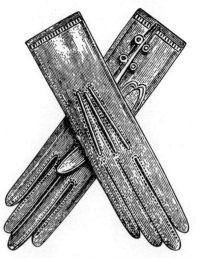

Q: *How did Lupin ensure that he could pull a matching pair of black or white gloves from the pouch in his pocket the first and only time he did so, without looking inside?*

The Problem with Coffee and Comfort?

ARSÈNE LUPIN WAS SITTING inside the Café des Westens in Berlin, drinking coffee with his new mathematician friend, David Hilbert.

"The coffee is not as good here as it once was . . ." Lupin commented, putting his cup down with displeasure.

"Ah, you see my friend, I agree with you and I asked the owner. Have you noticed the chairs are more comfortable?"

"I'll concede that, yes."

"Well, the owner said the sheer volume of complaints about the previous chairs had forced him to purchase all new ones, 100 chairs at 200 pfennigs or 2 Deutsche Marks a chair, a considerable expense out of his yearly budget."

"What has that to do with the coffee?"

"Well, he was buying Brazilian coffee, 10 DM for a 50 kg bag every week, but with this new expenditure he felt he had to cut corners somewhere. He did not want to compromise the food, so he bought cheaper coffee at 5 DM a bag."

Lupin shook his head. "I don't think that was the right decision."

"Perhaps. A week later he confessed to me that while before he was selling 200 cups of coffee a day at 10 pfennigs a cup, now he is selling 80 percent of that amount."

Hilbert leaned forward.

Q: "So, I ask you my friend: a) How much did he spend on the chairs? b) How much did he save changing the coffee type? And c) If he continues buying cheaper coffee for a year, will it compensate for buying the chairs if the lost profit from dissatisfied customers remains consistent?"

A Breath-taking
Interaction in Madrid

AN OFFICER IN MADRID'S Municipal Guard named Fidel de Vega had made the acquaintance of a man he suspected was Arsène Lupin, and decided to use his legendary experience and brain power when a mysterious robbery was committed.

"The facts are simple, Signor Gutiérrez," De Vega began. "The National Archaeological Museum here in Madrid has an excellent collection of Greek statuary and several cases of valuable ancient coins. They recently moved them because some fool printmaker moved next door and spilled nitric acid everywhere, and they didn't want anything damaged. Anyway, at 2 am yesterday during the changeover, the guard on duty was found unconscious. There was no sign of any physical assault, and the coins were gone. A nearby barred window had a large hole in the steel bars but no sign of any cutting. The statues were untouched except for some strange damage on the hair of one near the window, a blurring of detail."

Signor Gutiérrez considered this. "How did the guard feel when he awakened?"

"Light-headed and nauseous."

"Did he report any smells, strange tastes in his mouth?"

"No smells but he did feel somewhat sick, and there was a small vomit stain on his pillow. He said he tasted agua con gas, seltzer water, for some reason. He was too confused to explain what had happened."

"Hmmm, carbon dioxide. And the room is less ventilated. No evidence of the removed bars?"

"There were strange streaks of liquid metal on the wall. A sloppy workman, probably."

"But the marble statue was damaged, as if something . . . caustic had fallen upon it."

"Does this not sound like one of Arsène Lupin's crimes?"

Gutiérrez scoffed. "More like the work of a copycat, not a Lupin but a Liseron, a weed! Not a clever crime, but incompetent guards and a careless thief. Lucky the guard did not choke to death from his negligence and further besmirch the name of Lupin!"

Q: *What happened in the room?*

The Books of Doctor Pecqueux

L UPIN RECRUITED ME IN 1904. He had set his sights on a "Doctor"
Gaston Pecqueux, a buffoon, rich off the back of a curative tonic
wine called "Vin Pecqueux" that was nothing more than grape slops and
cod oil. Pecqueux had filled his gaudy mansion with expensive rubbish.
He also owned several valuable medical artefacts, stethoscopes, books
and skeletal remains.

"He sells poison to the gullible and then has the cheek to snap up all
these interesting items from actual doctors! Something must be done."

That something turned out to be that we would steal Pecqueux's copy of *De Humani Corporis Fabrica Libri Septem*, a set of seven books on human anatomy published in 1543.

They were actually printed on animal anatomy, the pages made of vellum, a form of parchment that used the membrane of calfskin. Although it was an ancient and difficult material, its durability compared to paper meant many old volumes had longer lifespans than newer ones.

Despite the doctor's supposedly secure house, we easily gained access by pretending to deliver a new collection of medical dictionaries (although Lupin had acquired them so cheaply that they weren't worth the paper they were printed on!).

Lupin was lifting the first volume of *De Humani* into a disguised crate when he suddenly turned it in his hands, feeling its weight. He peered up at a picture on the wall of a human corpse with its skin pulled outward and stretched tight, then flicked open the book and examined the pages.

"Not a hair out of place. Not a hair at all, in fact," he said. "Same colour on both sides."

"Forgeries?"

"The pages are thinly veiled references to Pecqueux's personality, lineage and even hygiene, written knowing he would never open the books . . . But I knew it was a forgery the second I picked it up, and as soon as I touched the pages."

He put a drop of ink on one of the pages and it grew in size.

"This doctor couldn't tell an animal from a vegetable. I think I might give Pecqueux a call tomorrow and arrange for a public reading of this fascinating tome . . ."

Q: *How could Lupin tell the book was a forgery without reading the contents?*

The Mysterious Secret
of Bouillabaisse

THE FAMILIES OF MARSEILLE take their personal bouillabaisse recipes very seriously, so it was a grave day when the patriarch of the Passedat family tearfully confessed to Arsène Lupin.

"Our recipe has been stolen! Taken from my mother's bedroom during her funeral!"

Lupin's lips pressed together firmly. Without their recipe, "Le Petit Nice Passedat" might fall into ruin.

"Who do you suspect?" he asked.

"Another chef! Juliette says she tasted it in another restaurant, but she cannot remember which evening. DuLonne cooked bouillabaise on Monday, Marceau cooked it on Tuesday, Merle cooked it on Wednesday, and Descouteux cooked it on Thursday."

"What fish did they use?" Lupin asked Juliette.

"Red gurnard and monkfish, of course!"

"Well then, on what day did the fishermen catch those fish?"

Lupin went to the docks and spoke to an observant elder.

"Red gurnard and monkfish, you say? Well, I remember at the beginning of the week they caught some sea urchins . . ."

"Yes, and?"

"They caught some good mussels one day. That was the day after they caught the weeverfish . . ."

"When did they catch the weeverfish?" asked Lupin, realizing there was no straight route to the truth here.

"They caught the weeverfish the same day they caught the John Dory!"

". . . But the red gurnard?"

The old man puffed on an antique-looking pipe that in other circumstances Lupin would gladly purloin.

"I remember . . . eating some delicious lobster they had just caught. Just the thing right in the middle of the week."

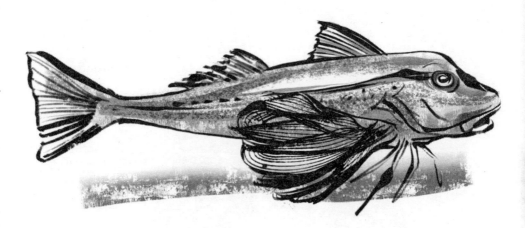

Lupin put his head in his hands.

"And they had some crab on one of the days too! But the red gurnard and monkfish . . ."

Lupin looked up.

". . . They were on the same day! I don't remember which. Two different fish every day. Strange."

Lupin gave the man some coins and stood up. He had all he needed.

> Q: a) What did they catch on what day?
> b) On what day was the bouillabaisse made?

The Art of the Steel

"ARSÈNE LUPIN HAS HAD a grudge against me for years!" blustered Ted Bainbridge to Mr. Finch, the head of his steel refinery, as they walked through the facility. "Ever since he tried to steal that statue from my house and got chased off by Magog!"

"Magog was a beautiful dog," said Mr. Finch kindly, holding his ever-present wrench, "like all of God's great creatures."

"Since then, he's been looking for a way to get revenge and sabotaging my refinery is the perfect way!" continued Bainbridge.

They went through the facility inspecting everything from the blast furnaces to the Bessemer converters, finding nothing until they reached a coke oven and heard a strange noise, almost like the squeak of a rusty gate or the horn of a motorcar. They approached, then suddenly heard a clanking noise behind them, like a thrown metal tool. They spun around swiftly.

"I saw Lupin!" Finch said. "Quick, you chase him, I'll stay here in case he returns."

"Nonsense!" said Bainbridge. "The exits are sealed."

The workers were assembled on the refinery floor and searched. Nothing was found except for tobacco and sweets. Finch had a handful of feathers in his pocket for some reason.

A little man named Bryant stepped forward. "I reckon this is a wild goose chase. This Loopin fella has got bigger eggs to hatch than messing around in our refinery," he said. The other workers nodded in agreement. Bryant was an old reliable.

"Mr. Bainbridge, I reckon there's just some spanner in the works and if you just let us shut down for a couple of hours it'll be sorted," he winked at Mr. Finch.

Bainbridge shut it down and two hours later production resumed with no problems, causing much happiness, with Mr. Finch beaming like a proud parent. Bryant came to work the next day claiming he'd been sick in bed for a week. And Bainbridge's house was now missing a valuable carriage clock.

Q: *Who was responsible for the problems, and why?*

Le Bourget Robbery Part I– The Vanishing Gold

LUPIN DID NOT COMMIT the Le Bourget robbery, but he did expose the perpetrators. Let me explain.

In 1923 Le Bourget was Paris's only airport. It had a sophisticated strong room in which to store any valuable items between flights. At 11 pm on the 15th of April the security guard on duty, who had the only keys, left to meet a flight. The locked room contained four boxes of gold sovereigns, value 500,000 francs. The boxes were especially designed to be heat-resistant, as the owner was irrationally concerned the sovereigns would melt in transit, even though gold only melts at 1,948 °F!

Hours later, during changeover, the guard's replacement found him slumped in a pool of blood. The room was empty.

No one at the airport had seen the robbers, but in a lucky coincidence a cyclist passing at 2 am had noted the registration on a bread van parked outside, 247-E, as it was the date of his wife's birthday. The only recent report of theft had been from the local foundry, nothing about bread vans, so the police visited the bakery where it was registered, considering it might be the hideout of the robbers.

Searching the property, they found nothing strange save a few traces of greyish lead paint splashed around. One of the policemen investigated the bread oven, burning his hands on it briefly as it was running at 2,000 °F, and came to a conclusion: they had baked loaves and hidden the gold in them!

The entire police force was employed in visiting the locations to which bread from the shop had been delivered. They ripped open the loaves, but not a single sovereign was found, the operation only enraging the local populace.

"Criminals everywhere and you are digging in bread like a rat!" growled an old woman.

"It is a stupid plan," said the officer with the fake moustache.

"Three times my apartment has been robbed! My door replaced, new iron bars installed on my windows and extra locks on everything." she lamented. "I could barely afford them. Lucky the men who did it had such a low price . . ."

Q: *What did the robbers do with the gold?*

The Lightning Thief

I N 1897 THE PARIS police received an anonymous letter and a film canister. The printed letter said, "I have captured the Grands Boulevards thief: Not in person, but on camera!"

(In reality the thief was Lupin, but he never admitted it because he was amused by the legend that arose.)

The police did not have their own film projector and so contacted the famous Lumière Brothers who had captured France's imagination with their films the previous year. They said they were too busy and gave the police the name of an amateur.

A drunk fellow named Michel Gagnant bumbled into the station and ran the film, which showed something incredible: a black-clad man moving across the rooftops with the speed of lightning, opening a window, and then out again seconds later with a bag full of loot! The police were astounded and terrified; this supernatural creature would not only be impossible to catch but also, what if it turned its terrifying speed toward the police themselves!

This consternation lasted for a day until an officer returned from seeing one of Georges Méliès' films and confirmed that the figure in the film was not actually moving at that speed, and it was simply a trick of playing a film that was made with 8 frames a second at a higher frame rate, such as 24 FPS. Gagnant had been too drunk to realize.

"At 24 FPS, the film travels through the projector at a rate of 456 mm per second." He continued, "The film must have been 3 minutes, but we saw only 1, so it must have been 8 frames a second!"

The cinephile police officer was sworn to secrecy as the police sought to hide their embarrassment and they covered the entire affair up. The legend of the lightning thief had already spread beyond the station and lasted for decades, and ironically was even the subject of several films!

Q: *If at 24 FPS film travels through a projector at 456 mm a second, what speed should it travel through at 8 FPS, and how much film must have moved through when it finished, keeping in mind it was a 3-minute-long film?*

Le Bourget Robbery Part II–
The Obvious Suspect

EDGARD BRET, AN OLD park cleaner, had recently bought himself a gold-plated wristwatch.

When younger, he had stolen a small watercolour painting and there had been reports of muggings in Parc Montsouris, where he worked. The police imprisoned him for interrogation. All he could mumble was, "The art man said it was a fair amount to pay and I thought so too, very fair, for fairies. Theodor who?"

Hours later they received a message saying, "Arsène Lupin knows Edgard Bret is innocent. Visit the house of Madame Idette Perrault."

Idette Perrault was a rich local recluse. The police did not like taking orders from Lupin, but they dutifully went to her house anyway. Madame Perrault was 87 but answered the door dressed like Little Red Riding Hood, grinning innocently.

"Soldiers from the king! Enter into the fairy kingdom . . ."

The "fairy kingdom" was her house, crammed floor to ceiling with fantasy objects, wax poisoned apples and enchanted chairs.

"Do you know Edgard Bret?" the chief officer asked, exasperated. Her face lit up.

"Once upon a time there was a sad young girl called Idette who lived in a fairy kingdom surrounded on all sides by a terrible cursed city. Idette only dared to venture into the city to meet her friends, the carriers of hope, in the forest of the mocking mice. But three trolls found Idette and wanted to steal her treasure! She was trapped, but suddenly a brave knight with a lance of bristles appeared and faced the trolls, frightening them away with his strong words and big beard. Idette was so grateful and gave the brave knight a kiss, then took him to the fairy kingdom and gave him Oberon and Titania as a gift!"

They declared the whole thing a waste of time and left. Lupin decided to act on his own, and 12 hours after a call to a shop at the Carré Rive Gauche, Bret was released without charge.

Q: *Where did Bret get the money?*

Riddle of the Dancing Seagull

I SAT NEXT TO LUPIN in a deck chair on the beach at Le Touquet. He sipped a citron pressé and sighed.

"At this moment the French authorities believe they are arresting me in Toulouse," he said matter-of-factly. "They set an obvious little trap with a rare stamp I have declared that I wanted. They didn't realize I already stole it three years ago and replaced it with a forgery . . . In Toulouse it is rainy and dull, and here I languish in the sunshine."

"Do you not tire of their pursuit?" I asked him.

"No, it is in their nature, as it is in mine, to avoid arrest. The seagull pursues the worm, the police pursue Lupin."

"You're calling yourself a worm?" I asked with amusement.

"Why not!" he said with a flourish. "Noble fellows, toiling underground, making the soil better for all. Worms move better when the soil is wet from the rain, and I move better when the world is stirred up with confusion and chaos!"

He pointed at the beach, where a group of seagulls were doing a strange dance on the sand, stamping their feet.

"Of course, the seagulls can always dance. The police are not as good at that."

"Why do they dance?" I asked, confused.

Q: *Why do seagulls dance on beaches?*

The Four Rooms of Felicite LeFleuve

IN 1929 FELICITE LEFLEUVE'S "perfumes for small dogs" were a sensation.

Every year she invited artists to her home in Cannes to paint, decorate or just smash things, so she could declare it a living work of art. The artists enjoyed a chance to have a wild party.

Several irreplaceable treasures had been broken during these parties, and Lupin decided this time he would save some of them.

That night artists known and unknown roved the halls with paintbrushes, chisels and hammers, Lupin disguised himself as a drunken Fauvist.

Four rooms held the items and also the most famous artists there.

An 18th-century Chantilly porcelain bowl was on a table in the room occupied by Walter Gropius, Bauhaus architect. Gropius was sitting in a chair soberly watching his wife Ise paint streaks of red across the wallpaper, occasionally glancing to admire the exquisite porcelain.

A 14th-century sword was on the wall in a room with Marcel Duchamp, surrealist artist and professional chess player. He was playing against a young man as chaos reigned around them. Duchamp didn't even notice the sword, but he had an open attitude to illegal conduct.

In the third room teams of artists chipped away at all four walls with their chisels, and at the heart Pablo Picasso was holding a rare Japanese puzzle box and attempting to open it, muttering that he thought he was done with cubism.

The final room seemed less a place of art and more a singing competition, as carousing youths took it in turns to open bottles of wine from LeFleuve's well-appointed cellar. They didn't realize that one of the bottles they discarded was a magnum of champagne from 1811.

Drinking a glass of whisky nearby, smiling politely but otherwise not engaging, was Edward Hopper, memorizing faces for possible inclusion in a future painting.

Suddenly a group of burly hired thugs enters the house looking for Lupin. Someone tipped LeFleuve off!

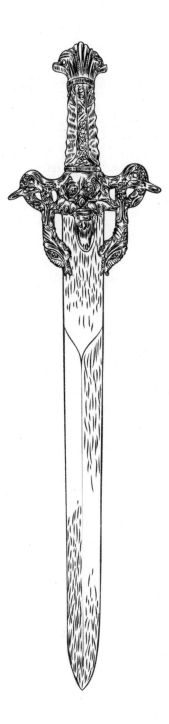

Q: *Lupin can only steal one item. Which one does he have the best chance of successfully taking without getting caught?*

The Chagrin of Chez Darien

A T THE HEIGHT OF a particular swell of Lupinmania in 1904, a restaurant in Lyon named Chez Darien decided to promote itself with a simple idea: if at the end of your meal you would declare to the entire restaurant, "I am Arsène Lupin!" you would receive 20 percent off the cost!

This promotion lasted for only 45 minutes, however, when a waggish fellow, after enjoying a huge meal with many courses and several fine wines totalling 44 francs, shouted "I am Arsène Lupin!"—the first to do so.

"Ah, monsieur, you shall receive 20 percent off!" the waiter declared.

"I am Arsène Lupin!" the man declared again.

"We heard you the first time, monsieur . . ." said the waiter uncertainly.

"I know, I am getting another 20 percent off!" the man said, grinning.

"Oh no, monsieur, it is only a single discount . . ."

"It does not say that in the advertisement!" said the man, brandishing a newspaper.

The owners reluctantly agreed that this was the case, as the man continued shouting this now dreaded phrase.

Q: *How many times can this man receive 20 percent off before the amount can no longer be measured in centimes, of which there are 100 to a franc? The 20 percent is taken off each new amount, not the original 44 franc amount.*

The Tomb of Robert d'Argent

"GRAVE ROBBERS ARE JACKALS, fiends," Lupin said to me as he began cracking open the wall of the tomb of Robert d'Argent with a sledgehammer. "But anyone who takes something of beauty and shuts it away with themselves forever is worse. The dead cannot appreciate anything. Once I have retrieved the Medici bracelet, I will personally have this tomb repaired—to a better standard, in fact."

The wall crumbled and the coffin was exposed. Lupin carefully pried it open only to find it empty, not only of the bracelet but of any corpse. The look on his face was a mix of frustration and excitement at this new challenge. Feeling inside the lining, he found a piece of parchment. Written in Latin it said:

"To those who intended to steal the bracelet, please be informed that I am elsewhere, and this coffin contained a deadly gas . . ."

We cleared the tomb immediately, and after Lupin established the second part was a cruel joke, he returned and began pondering the bracelet's location. The note had no clues, but the wall of the tomb had D'Argent's family tree engraved, and there was a mark on one of the branches.

"Perhaps this is who got the Medici bracelet. Not such a hoarder after all. But who is it?"

The tomb was 400 years old, and beyond the legend of the bracelet, records of D'Argent's life were spotty.

At the archives Lupin learned that Robert d'Argent had a sister called Plaisance. Later he learned Plaisance was the mother of a child named Quentin, and he also learned of a woman called Sylvie d'Argent, the daughter of Robert. Another book revealed a Terese who was the sister of Plaisance and had a son, Uriel.

Q: What is the relation between Uriel, Quentin and Sylvie?

Napoleon's Sword

I WAS ONLY A REGULAR house breaker; never thought I had any particular skill in it, but then this bloke named Lupin sends me a message via a carrier pigeon of all things and I meet him in my local pub. Here's this smart-looking French geezer sitting on one of the stained old benches like he was born to it, drinking a pint of milk stout.

"Reginald, you don't know it, but you have the hands of an angel. Fifty-four houses broken into and not one window smashed. I need your sensitivity, mon frère," he says.

"What's the job?" I ask.

He lobs a couple of old manuscripts on the table. "Napoleon's sword. Solid gold hilt and a fire-gilded blade. Recovered at the site of his greatest victory. It is being transported, and ironically will be most vulnerable to your incredible hands when it will be briefly stored in a train station that is named after that self-same victory."

He knew my answer would be yes, otherwise he wouldn't have told me, but I couldn't figure out which station it was going to be, although I had a few ideas . . .

Q: *At which station will the sword be vulnerable?*
   a) King's Cross.
   b) Gare de Lyon.
   c) Waterloo.
   d) Gare d'Austerlitz.

Le Bourget Robbery Part III– The Betrayal

AFTER A TIP-OFF FROM Lupin, the police arrested air pilot Phillipe Morel, locksmith Absalon Fournier and criminal Guy Tasse.

Two months earlier, Morel had plied the security guard with alcohol, borrowed the keys and elicited Fournier to make copies. Morel owed money to Tasse, hence his involvement. They snuck in to steal it while the guard was occupied, but they took too long and attacked him upon his return.

Lupin had exposed them because he disliked being associated with such sloppiness and unnecessary violence.

None of the suspects denied committing the robbery, but each claimed that they had not struck the guard. Tasse said Fournier did it, clutching rosary beads in his hand as if for comfort. "I will not confess to this!" he declared. "I confess only to one man."

Fournier passionately denied it: "I cannot stand the sight of blood!"

They all also claimed not to have the gold! They had stored it in Fournier's workshop while Tasse arranged for its sale.

Tasse claimed he was meeting his contact, Fournier claimed to have gone to the infamously gory and violent Grand Guignol theatre, and Morel insisted he'd ventured to a local bar to drown his guilt, though he said he drowned it so well he could not recall the bar's name. "There were no seats, and the floor was dirty. I could hear water nearby, and traffic and people passing above me. There were all these ashen-faced people scowling at me, their faces stony. I think some of them had horns." The police concluded he'd spent the evening with the "green fairy."

When all three returned at 11 pm as planned, the shop's windows were smashed, and the gold stolen. As the only people who knew where it was, one of them must have been the culprit.

Fournier had a stamped ticket from the performance. None of the local bar and drinking establishments remembered Morel having visited them, so his alibi was unproven. Tasse's contact denied having met him, though he said he had seen him walking toward Sacré-Coeur in Montmartre that night. With no one reliable to vouch for him, Tasse was clearly the main suspect.

Q: *Who attacked the guard, and who stole the gold?*

Lupin Escapes the Boars

LUPIN HAD TO MOVE fast and think fast. The Boars were hot on his trail! Formed in 1912 especially to track him and crack him, they had blown his network, raided his hiding places and had extensive knowledge of his primary disguises. It would be thrilling if it wasn't the most scared he had been in years. He had to throw them off his track and find a place to rest and regroup. But he also had to signal to his only remaining trusted ally where he would be, without sending messages in any form!

He looked at a news headline about the "BOARS," their name an acronym coming from "Brigade Officielle pour Appréhender Raoul Serane," which was his most common pseudonym at this time. They were so popular the public did not even mind that their name was in English! But it did give him an idea . . .

Over the next few days, Lupin journeyed extensively, and the Boars were on him every step of the way, with the national papers trumpeting every move!

First to Lille via passenger train, then a short run to Ypres on a stolen motorcycle. Lupin hopped a heavy goods train to Orléans before heading south and seemingly stopping in Nice. At each step the newspapers told the tale of the Boars' close pursuit and in Nice they really thought they had him, but when 50 men raided his hotel room he had gone, and there was no trace of his next destination.

However, his ally knew exactly where to find him, as easily as if he had sent letters . . .

Q: *In which French city is Lupin hiding?*

The Death of Frans Sonne

B Y 1934, LUPIN FOUND himself wanting to commit more exotic and esoteric robberies. One such theft was his acquisition of one of the few existing versions of the famous Schmidt optical reflecting telescope from Frans Sonne, a rich industrialist who kept it on his balcony and used it essentially as a toy to entertain people at parties. As the first son of Reiner Sonne, the notorious bank cartel leader, Frans particularly liked showing people the first planet from the sun through the telescope, as he felt a strange kinship with it.

So, when Lupin found him dead on the floor of his apartment, poisoned, he had a hunch what had happened.

A shattered glass of what appeared to be cognac lay next to the body. Frans's face looked unnaturally flushed and red, especially around the cheeks. He was also only wearing a bathrobe. Noting that his personal sauna was open, Lupin went inside and concluded he had been in there and stumbled out. Taking note of a broken thermometer on the wall, Lupin had a thought and quickly ran out of the sauna, returning with a handkerchief across his face and opening up the little stove to find a particular element on the coals.

This could have been an accident, he thought, but then remembered that Sonne's servant, a fast and efficient young man nicknamed Hermès, had recently been dismissed by him and accused of theft.

Knowing Sonne's not-so-secret fascistic associations, Lupin would not help the police with this case, but he did note the ironic connection between three key elements of this situation . . .

Q: *What is the connection between Frans's favourite planet, his murderer and the method of his murder?*

The Fuses of Las Fallas

L UPIN USUALLY PREFERRED NOT to use explosives to open safes, but this particular safe could not be cracked by other means, largely because his copycat impersonator, the Liseron, had already attempted to break it open and had caused the mechanism inside to seize up.

As Lupin was using the festival of Las Fallas here in Valencia as cover for this theft, there was no time for an alternative—dynamite was his only option. He attached it to the enormous safe and extracted an extremely long fuse from his bag, one that he knew took an hour to burn.

But as he did this, his pocket watch fell and shattered on the floor! This was a problem as he knew that in 45 minutes he was needed at the main ceremony in his persona as a visiting businessman and donor. The loud bangs and shouts of the crowd provided good cover for his use of the explosives but would also mean he could not hear the chimes of the local clock, and he mustn't leave this room before time or be discovered.

He pulled his two spare one-hour fuses from his bag. Both fuses burned at an inconsistent rate, but he knew a trick that would allow him to know exactly when 45 minutes had passed . . .

Q: *How did he measure 45 minutes? He could light one or both of the fuses, at one or both ends at the same time.*

Bureau de Change

I N THE EARLY DAYS of his career Lupin did not have the vast sums of money he had later accrued, and therefore when a seasoned con man Lupin knew named Baptise Bureau was captured and imprisoned, he did not have the resources to either break or bribe him out.

"I have the money in my Swiss account . . ." Bureau wrote in a short message he had smuggled out, ". . . but I cannot write down the numbers or others here will help themselves to what I have saved. I trust you will be clever enough to deduce the answers from my statements."

And Lupin was clever enough, in the main, to be able to pick up references to the numbers of places they both knew, the ages of friends or family, and other references. But he had difficulty with one of the final numbers, for which Bureau had written:

"Multiply me by myself and you will get the equivalent of adding me to myself."

Lupin pondered this and noted that in the margins of this clue Bureau had added various symbols that when translated referred to the numbers 17, 4, 12, 80, 2, 90 and 12. From this he assumed it was one of those. But which?

Q: Which number is the answer to the puzzle?

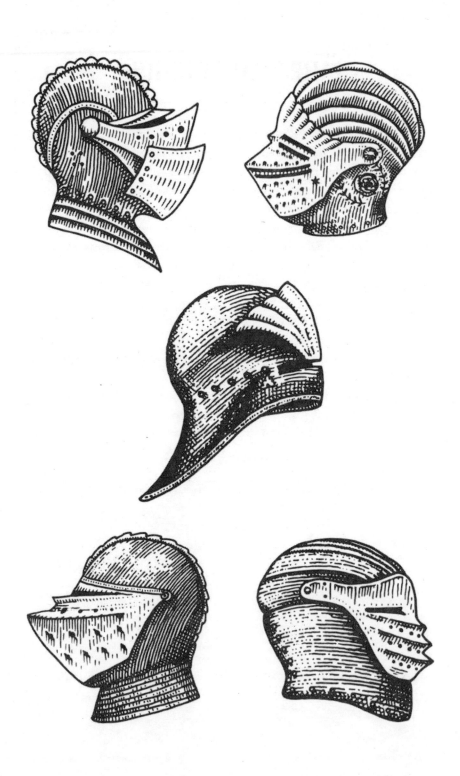

The Five Knights

THE CHATEAU DE BERGERAC was very charming and had some interesting historical details, and Lupin resolved to come back for a tour when he wasn't being chased by all of its guards. It was medieval by origin but had been altered in 1707 by the current Duke, who was equally beguiled by Arthurian legend and Newtonian science.

Lupin entered the famous chapel, decorated with five tapestries of legendary knights who had inspired the Chateau's owner: Jean de Dijon, Armand de Blanc, Phillipe de Violette, Jean d'Vert and Barthélémy de Rougemont.

The common visitor would be unaware that behind each tapestry lay a door. One of the five doors led to a secret escape route, while the others were said to activate traps and mechanisms that would bring about the destruction of the castle itself! No one had ever dared attempt to open any of the doors for reasons of fear and superstition.

Lupin had spent several weeks impersonating a researcher at the national archives and had finally found a lost manuscript, a riddle that held the answer to the correct door:

"First you take the mimosa's hue,
add this to the brightest blue.
Take the fruit that grows from a seed,
add to the shade of envy and greed.
Mix the dye that the Orient makes
to the flower from Toulouse that in February wakes.
Take what you have and mix them all
with the hue of the blood that was spilled in the fall.
The colour you've made is the path that's right,
provided that you see the light."

Q: *Which door is the correct one—Jean de Dijon, Armand de Blanc, Phillipe de Violette, Jean d'Vert or Barthélémy de Rougemont?*

The Countess's Conundrum

THE SWORD POINT WAS expertly held to Lupin's neck, a drop of his blood at its tip. The arm that held it was that of Josephine Balsamo, the self-proclaimed Countess of Cagliostro, Lupin's sworn enemy and occasional paramour.

Her eyes danced with mischief at his predicament. He tried his best to look calm and uncaring, but he knew she would happily make him a human scabbard.

"Arsène, are you stealing from me again?" she said playfully, her eyes darting for a second to the bags of gold coins sliding around on the floor of the train carriage as it raced along at incredible speed.

"I have to admit I didn't know these were yours," he said carefully as his Adam's apple danced around the blade's end.

"Well actually, they aren't yet, but I was just about to steal them."

"In that case, I will bid you adieu . . ."

The two armed men behind him made it clear an exit was not a possibility.

"Oh Arsène, I will give you a little challenge. If the next thing you say is true, I will immediately throw you off this moving train onto the jagged rocks. And if the next thing you say is a lie, I will instantly gut you like a salmon."

She tightened her grip on the sword.

"But if you somehow manage to confound me, you are free to go. Well?"

Q: *What can Lupin say that will lead to Josephine releasing him?*
a) "You will release me.
b) "This is not a lie."
c) "You will gut me like a salmon."

The Pétanque Wager

T HE MOST FRUSTRATING PART of any robbery or other escapade for Lupin was not the act itself but the sometimes tedious business of information gathering, which often involved spending a lot of time in different disguises and personas. Sometimes Lupin found it enjoyable, like the seven months he spent as a baker in a small village in the Occitane, and other times it was dull, like the time he spent as a Pétanque instructor for a Belgian millionaire whose name he could not even remember to relate to me. Lupin achieved this by seeing an actual Pétanque instructor on the days he wasn't working for the millionaire, ensuring he was always one lesson ahead.

Annoyingly, the millionaire, usually a garrulous man, had become uncharacteristically tight-lipped about the security arrangements for his upcoming ball, at which his wife intended to wear the fabled Necklace of the Sands. Then Lupin realized the egotistical man was accustomed to feeling better than everyone and felt Lupin's superior technique at Pétanque diminished him somehow. At this point, Lupin played worse and worse as a way of making the millionaire believe he was racing ahead of him in skill.

"Oho, off your form again today, my friend?" the millionaire boasted as he won another round. "Perhaps you might be interested in laying down a little money to see who succeeds in the next few rounds? Three francs per round?"

Lupin agreed. In the course of the day, he managed to extract the information he needed, winning two of the bets, and the millionaire ended his lesson 18 francs richer.

Q: How many rounds of Pétanque did they play?

The Calendar Bridge

LUPIN THOUGHT HE HAD sworn off stealing from ancient castles or catacombs that had complex puzzle-based traps within, but every few months or so he'd hear of another exciting legendary artefact, and he had to try and get it. This is how he found himself standing before a strange stone bridge made up of octagonal tiles, each marked with random numbers in Roman numerals from 1–9. His assistant Reginald was lagging behind, trying to get rid of Coleb, an opportunistic and violent American fortune hunter who had trailed them to this place. Luckily, thanks to acquiring an illuminated manuscript from the British Museum, Lupin knew the correct tiles to step on to avoid falling to his death, and made his way across nimbly, if carefully.

Reginald now appeared, out of breath and dishevelled but unharmed, and Lupin was about to shout to him when Coleb appeared, thankfully now unarmed. But how could Lupin tell Reginald which steps to use without Coleb then also knowing the code?

Remembering Coleb's ignorance of French, Lupin shouted out "Septembre! Juin! Mai! Avril! Fevrier! Fevrier! Décembre!"

Reginald was at first confused, but then stepped on number 9 and was able to traverse the bridge. Coleb fell to a sad but inevitable end.

Q: *How did Lupin's words help Reginald know the path?*
And what were the numbers he had to step on?

Roulette of the Russian

L UPIN HAD TO ADMIT that the Russian guard had tied his ropes very
well. Even a master of escape like Lupin had very little opportunity
to pull them apart. The chair was more likely to break than the ropes,
and in fact that might be what Lupin had to do, but for the moment he
was stuck.

The guard sat opposite him, a grizzled, beaten-down man, his
dead-eyed expression indicative of many years of boring duties at this
Siberian outpost. Lupin hoped that maybe having different company
after all these years might have lifted his spirits. But it didn't seem to be
the case.

"Let's play a little game," the man said, picking up his Modèle revolver.
He emptied it of bullets, then put a single one back in the chambers.
Lupin had heard of this game and could honestly say he had never
wanted to play it.

The man spun the chambers, pointed the gun at Lupin and pulled the
trigger . . . CLICK!

"Ah, what a shame," the man said. Lupin had almost managed to snap
the back of the chair with his arms.

The man held the gun up again. "Shall I pull the trigger immediately?
Or would you like me to spin the chambers again first?"

Q: Would Lupin have a better chance if the man spins the chambers, or not?

The Tale of LeCanard

OSTENTATIOUS IDIOTS WILL NEVER go out of fashion, and Eben LeCanard was definitely one of them. He took the entire fortune he had inherited from his father and had it converted into gold sovereigns, which he stored in a special facility all piled on top of each other. He claimed he could not truly appreciate the money unless he could see it every day.

Of course, this was a big target for robbers, and so the facility had one of the biggest and most overzealous security forces in the world. For this reason, everyone assumed Arsène Lupin would soon be calling.

Then one night LeCanard passed through the many security checkpoints and entered the vault. All the coins seemed to be there and seemed to be perfect, but when he looked at them there was something wrong: they each had a cartoon of a winking duck upon them! Looking further, he found that they were not gold, but gilded tungsten!

"Who else could it have been but Lupin?" This is what Lupin asked himself that morning, as it was not him. Canard's vault was too obvious a target for him.

"Perhaps it was that Liseron," he mused as he read the newspaper story.

"It's obvious the guards were bribed, but who had the skill to make such excellent forgeries?"

Looking at the newspaper photo, he realized something. There were four types of coins with four different number values, but unlike with the original coins, you could create the values 1–10 with a minimum of one coin and a maximum of two! It spoke to a master forger with a wicked sense of humour, the creator of the fake medical book.

"Le Style," he said. It rhymes with steal.

Q: *What are the four values of the coins?*

The Impossible Leap

THE LONG-DEPARTED URIEL D'ARGENT had a magnificent 53 m (164 ft) tall tower built in tribute to him at the edge of a forest in the Camargue. It commemorated a military victory that never actually happened, and ended up being his final resting place instead. His coffin lay in the foyer at the entrance, then a spiral staircase led all the way up the inside of the tower to a viewing gallery at the top, recently refurbished with velvet curtains. It is this way that Lupin ran when he was discovered by the men assigned to guard the tower.

Lupin had evidently intended to get in and out with the portion of the bracelet without anyone being aware of his presence. He researched the two guards, Jean and Anton, and found them to be fundamentally lazy people who normally slept all through their shifts, but had neglected to examine their more recent activities, and in the past couple of weeks they had taken to playing cards for money in the evening. Anton was losing so badly at poker to Jean that his ears were attentive for any reason to distract from this fact.

"You're such a bad liar . . ." Jean said to Anton as he won another hand.

"Wait, what's that?" Anton shouted at the infinitesimal sounds of Lupin picking the foyer's lock.

They ran into the room to find Lupin removing the bracelet piece from the ceremonial coffin, as well as a bag of gold sovereigns, and Jean managed to quickly get behind Lupin, blocking his access to the door.

Taking the only alternative route, Lupin began sprinting up the spiral staircase with Anton in hot pursuit. Jean followed after, slightly out of breath as he was much less fit than Anton. When he arrived in the viewing gallery, he found Anton staring open-mouthed like a stuffed haddock at the balcony. Lupin was nowhere to be seen.

"Where is he?" asked Jean, looking around confused.

"He leapt over the balcony!" said Anton with wonder. "I tried to stop him, but he dove forward and went straight over! And yet there is no sign of him!"

They both peered over the balcony but there was no body sprawled on the ground, nor was he dangling by his fingertips.

Q: *How did Lupin enact his miraculous escape?*

The Wall of Theseus

D URING ONE OF HIS occasional times in prison, Lupin had as his cellmate a wild, untamed beard with a peculiar man attached behind it.

"So, you're the famous master thief, are you? Well, I have a brilliant plan for you."

"Really?" said Lupin, always open to new possibilities.

"We steal the Great Wall of China!"

"Oh."

The man scrambled forward.

"No, listen, listen, it sounds impossible, yes, but what is the Great Wall made of? Bricks! All you have to do is go there and take a single brick and replace it with an identical one! You hide that, and then return and do it again! Brick by brick you are stealing the wall, and no one will ever notice!"

"Ingenious."

"There is but one flaw in my plan."

"The number of bricks?"

"No! I have calculated there are about three billion, eight hundred and seventy-three million bricks, that's not so many."

"The time taken to hide them?"

"No! We will take each brick to Mongolia; it only takes seven hours to travel there!"

"Is it not possible to get the replacement bricks?"

"No, they can be secured from a special factory that is also in Mongolia, but they make them in batches of 5,000 and it takes them two days to make each batch."

"Then what is the flaw?" asked Lupin, amused.

"Finding a buyer! My previous cellmate said he would purchase it, but he offered to pay in moon cheese. If I'm honest, I think he was a bit touched in the head . . ."

Q: *Assuming there are 3,873,000,000 bricks in the Great Wall of China, it takes seven hours to get to Mongolia and after every 5,000 bricks you must wait two days for a new batch, if you only take one brick at a time, how many years would it take to replace the entire wall, rounding down?*

The Torment Machine of Baron von der Leyen und zu Hohengeroldseck

L UPIN CROUCHED BEFORE THE diabolical contraption. It was a mass of pipes and wheels, levers and chutes. Yet another of the Baron von der Leyen und zu Hohengeroldseck's Torment Machines. At its core lay three different boxes, A, B and C, which Lupin knew contained either real rubies, high-quality forgeries, or a mix of both.

The machine required the user to submit various body parts for the infliction of pain and suffering, at the end of which one of the boxes would be released at random. Lupin, of course, had found an alternative, and had managed to persuade one of the Baron's assistants to label the boxes for him. All he had to do was literally lever the box off the machine and then dive through the window before its inbuilt anti-tamper mechanism activated the stick of dynamite at the base.

Just one problem: moments before he entered the room, the assistant spitefully cried, "Actually, I've given every box THE WRONG LABEL!" and locked the door, running off to find the Baron and his guards.

Lupin looked at the crudely written notes saying: a) "REAL," b) "FAKE," and c) "BOTH." He saw only one possibility, his Plan B: Eurydice.

He removed Eurydice the pygmy marmoset from her special carrier. She was trained to move through any number of small spaces and retrieve valuable objects. He sent her into the machine, and she quickly made her way to Box c) "BOTH." She then returned, a little oily but unharmed, and put a single ruby into Lupin's hand. Lupin peered at it carefully: it was a forgery. He now knew exactly where the real rubies were.

Q: *Which box has the real rubies, and how does Lupin know?*

The Shattered Glass

THE LEGENDARY SCULPTOR ALEJANDRO Woras considered his greatest work to be a tiny wax statue of Eve. His will stipulated the creation of an underground shrine, closed to visitors, and whose custodians could only open it once a year.

After opening innumerable iron doors, the custodians would enter a long concrete room, at the other end of which was the statue behind toughened glass. It was contained in a special bottle that Woras had created himself—strong and flawless. It was open at the top to keep the wax dry but there were no other entrances and exits, and the ventilation shaft above the bottle was so small that nothing but a tiny object like a seed of a plant could get through. The bottle stood on a special concrete plinth. The outside area was carefully patrolled, and a guard had only two months previously captured a youth attempting to drop a coin into the top of the ventilation shaft, the shielding of which had apparently been damaged previously.

That year the custodians entered and were stunned to see the bottle was smashed, its contents seemingly gone. No sign of forced entry. Just a scattering of dirt on the floor with some tangled root-like matter. Concerned about making things worse, they called the insurance company, and when the investigator arrived, he insisted on entering first.

"Statue in a bottle?" he muttered with bemusement, peering around the back of the podium. He moved the glass pieces around with his foot.

"Careful, monsieur!" uttered a custodian. "That is Master Woras's work."

"Sorry, I just did not want to cut my fingers," he said. "Why's the floor wet?"

"It should not be; the ventilation is carefully designed to keep this room cool and dry," the man said with consternation.

"Looks like it's been dripping water from the ceiling," the insurance agent said. "Hope you don't mind me eating my apple, I didn't have breakfast," he added, although the thing he began munching on was brown and oddly large and lumpy, rather more like a potato than an apple.

"Why does all the glass look like it has exploded outward?" asked a custodian. "And where did all this dirt come from?"

"It is not my place to comment on how badly you keep this place clean, monsieur," said the insurance agent, walking out of the door.

It was only two days after he left that the custodians received a message from Lupin revealing he was the insurance agent, thanking them both for the opportunity to take the statue, and for his breakfast.

Q: *How did Lupin break the glass bottle?*

The Church Clock

T HE POLICE COULDN'T BELIEVE their luck! For once they actually had something. While chasing a cow that had escaped from a field, a rural policeman had accidentally found a message from Lupin to one of his compatriots, instructions for some kind of upcoming robbery, apparently connected with the graveyard of the church in Auvillar, a small village in the Occitane.

The note read: "AM is the hour. PM is the minute. Five steps for each time. Begin with Evonne Bellerose. 12:00 am. 3:00 pm. 7:45 pm. 9:23 am. 4:00 pm. 12:51 am. 9:03 am."

In the graveyard the police found the grave of Evonne Bellerose at the bottom right of the square-shaped area. They also realized a surprising number of famous people were buried here, such as Acelet Blanc the former chanteuse at the middle left of the graveyard, Louvel Danieu the novelist at the top left, and Jean Lambert the former Defence Minister at the top right.

They staked out the graveyard, taking it in shifts waiting for Lupin's accomplice to appear. When after a few days nothing happened and they grew impatient, they decided to only stake it out at the times he mentioned. But when the policeman arrived for his 9:03 am shift, he found one of the graves already dug up! Why would Lupin's assistant visit at a different time?

Perhaps they were not meant to be times at all?

Q: *Whose grave was dug up, and why?*

The Deadly Jar

QUENTIN D'ARGENT'S GRAVE WAS different from that of many other Frenchman's, as in his life he had developed a mania for the culture of Egypt, long before the more recent craze spurred by Carter's excavation of Tutankhamun.

In fact, looking around at the fake decorations and the sarcophagus, Lupin would have to say that if D'Argent had never been inside an actual Pharaoh's tomb, then the person who designed this had. It was, however, difficult to look around with the knife held to his throat.

This knife was wielded by the American graverobber Coleb, who had survived his fall from the bridge and had trailed Lupin here, determined to get revenge.

"You're a decent man, Mr Coleb," Lupin began, knowing this wasn't true but that Coleb liked to believe it was. "So, what say we fight hand to hand, like gentlemen?"

Coleb considered this. "Sure, why not?" he drawled nastily, "but first, I reckon you need a snack."

He picked up one of the jars from the masses arrayed at the wall and handed it to Lupin.

"Here. Eat all a'this, and then we can fight, just fists."

Lupin peered at the jar. It was food left for D'Argent to eat in the afterlife, but it would be over 200 years old. Coleb was relying on crippling stomach pains and possible food poisoning to take the edge off Lupin's martial ability.

Then he noted the hexagonal shape on the jar, and opening it, sniffed the contents. Smiling, Lupin grabbed a nearby spoon and ate the glutinous contents swiftly. Then, unaffected by any pains or poisoning, he easily beat Coleb in the fist fight.

Q: *What was in the jar, and why didn't it poison or otherwise affect Lupin?*

The Hair of Mélusine

I OFTEN ASKED LUPIN WHY he had not conducted more business in Australia. Although it was a long journey to get there, that had not necessarily stopped him before, time being merely another coin he was willing to trade for the opportunity of acquiring treasures.

"I did go there once," he said, staring into the distance. "There was an illicit offshore casino, a cruise ship. The owner would bring his guests to it with a speedboat. I was quite young, and my compatriot and I thought it easy to make our way there in a small canoe, stealthily, dressed entirely in black.

"Once we arrived, we climbed out of the canoe and into the water, wary of toxic Australian creatures like jellyfish or the venomous stonefish. My friend briefly went under but emerged seeming fine. But as we infiltrated the groups of gamblers, my otherwise happy-go-lucky friend became desperately despondent, paranoid and panicking with despair, grabbing my shoulders and shouting in my face:

"Oh my god, Lupin, the hair!! The hair of Mélusine!! It entangled me; the world is a black pit of hopelessness!"

He got increasingly frantic. Luckily the other guests assumed he was either drunk, losing money, or both, but I had to manhandle him into a storage room to try to quieten him. He was getting worse, clawing at his clothes. I tried splashing water on his face, but nothing. Suddenly one of the waiters was standing behind us.

"Your mate go in the water?" he asked, sombrely.

I could only nod, and the waiter unscrewed a jar of pickled eggs on a nearby shelf and bizarrely threw the contents at my friend. This somehow seemed to calm him.

"Irukandji. Not everything just stings; sometimes they affect your mind too. Get him to the medical bay, give him some morphine. Then I suggest you get off this bloody ship."

"We followed his advice and my friend survived, but after that I have preferred not to go there. There are too many dangerous mysterious things, even for Lupin."

Q: *What happened to his friend?*

The Vanishing Franc

LUPIN VISITED HIS MATHEMATICIAN friend David Hilbert again, taking a walk together in the gardens of the Tuileries.

"You are a person who has a great interest in making money disappear . . ." Hilbert commented cheekily.

"Money never disappears, it is simply transported somewhere else," Lupin retorted.

"Is that correct? I heard a story that suggests otherwise. A friend of mine had dinner with two of his closest companions. It cost 30 francs all told, and so they paid 10 each. Then just after they had left, the maître d' realized he had overcharged—the true price was 25 francs! He gave the kitchen boy 5 francs and told him to run into the street and give it to them, as they could not have gone far.

"But it seems the kitchen boy realized that 5 francs cannot be divided by three, and as my friend did not know the true amount, the boy decided instead to give them each 1 franc and keep 2 for himself.

"However, as they each were given 1 franc, that means they only paid 9 francs per person, which makes 27 francs. If the kitchen boy has kept 2 francs, this makes a total of 29 francs! But they paid 30! What do you think?"

"I think it's strange you said your friend didn't know about the true cost of the food, and yet he related it to you," said Lupin, smiling.

Q: What happened to the missing franc?

Chaton's Horde

ONE OF LUPIN'S LONG-TIME associates, a master safecracker and cat-burglar, had passed away. Lupin was amazed that a man who was so fond of explosives that he lost a hand and two toes to their usage had in the end succumbed to the simple hardships of old age. In his will he insisted that Lupin take personal possession of his most valued items.

Lupin entered Chaton's fastidiously neat but spartan apartment. Chaton was famously vain about his appearance but hated glittery gewgaws. The room was sparsely decorated with no sign of the many treasures Lupin knew he had stolen during his long life. There was supposedly a pet in here somewhere, Chaton's beloved Manx cat Brujon, but Lupin saw no sign of him.

After some careful searching, Lupin found what he sought: a secret panel under the corner of the carpet, allowing access to a separate room. It required a number code, ten rotatable brass dials. LeMarchand had written him a guide, though of course he had written it in code as a challenge for his greatest pupil.

"HANDS, FEET, TAILS, EYES, TOES. Me first."

Lupin quickly intuited its meaning. The vain Chaton had used his own body as the source for the numbers. And yet, the code required ten digits and there were only five options. Furthermore, for some reason the dials could go all the way up to 20.

Suddenly Brujon darted out from behind a chair and attacked Lupin's leg with his claws, as sneaky as his owner. A natural brawler, his single eye gazed malevolently at Lupin (he had lost the other in a fight with a wolf, Chaton claimed).

Lupin, thinking, now knew the entire code.

Q: What is the ten-digit code?

The Funeral of Simon de Sauter

L UPIN PREFERRED NOT TO attend funerals in general, but he made an exception for Chaton. He was amused to see he was far from the only person in disguise at this ceremony, in fact the priest himself was actually a master forger.

As he listened to the eulogy, Lupin reflected on one of the most ridiculous funerals he had attended as a young man. In the 1890s there was a famous performer called Simon de Sauter, the jumping clown. His act was entirely composed of him reciting nursery rhymes while leaping two-legged in the air for 15 minutes, dressed as Pierrot. Somehow this was considered amazing entertainment and he was much feted, although many Englishmen claimed he had simply stolen the act of J.H. Stead (De Sauter countered that he had thought of it first, and could jump for five minutes longer than Stead . . .)

As he aged, the jumping became more difficult for De Sauter, and he eventually retired, seemingly in squalor in a run-down block of apartments, and then died soon after. All his entertainer friends were horrified that his family might not even be able to pay for his funeral, and so staged a series of benefit concerts to raise the necessary funds.

Armand Castelmary, the legendary opera singer, reprised his famous role as Don Carlos for one night, and made the most money. Paul-Marie Verlaine was suffering ill health himself but managed to earn a third of what Castelmary did with a public reading of his works. Aline Permont, the nightclub chanteuse, performed four nights, earning the same amount each night which combined was double that of Verlaine. Sylvaine Ardout, the whistling contortionist, was much less popular, but still earned some money. And Jehan Pelletier, the mime, earned the third largest amount, as much as Ardout and Verlaine combined.

Then days before the funeral they learned that De Sauter had in fact hoarded 5,000 francs! The money, unneeded, would be returned to the masses, and it was done at his actual funeral, the first and last Lupin had seen that involved all the mourners receiving a payment!

Q: *The amounts of money raised were, in rising order, 30, 40, 70, 80 and 120.*
Who earned what?

The Bouncing Ball

HERMAN VOLET, HABERDASHER, WAS laying out some valuable fabrics when BAM! Something hard and fast hit his window at great velocity. If he had not had new reinforced windows installed (to muffle the noise from the piano store opposite), it would surely have smashed. Instead it left only a small crack.

Other shop owners along the row of streets faced the same strange disturbance, something medium-sized but fast and hard bouncing off or near their windows, breaking several before it came to rest in the road. The shopkeepers all ran out to peer at it: it was an Indian rubber ball! One of such ferocious bounciness as to ricochet from window to window with incredible speed.

Once they returned to their stores, many of the shopkeepers found them vandalized, their money stolen. It was a diabolical ruse, and one name was on everyone's lips. . .

"Lupin," said Lupin, shaking his head in dismay. "This ridiculous escapade gets laid at my feet. But Lupin has no time to have gangs of youths robbing poor shopkeepers! This is Liseron, that Lupin impersonating weed again."

Lupin put out a declaration to the newspapers saying as such!

Then he was amazed when the next day the newspapers printed a rebuttal from Liseron himself! "I have decided to step from your increasingly small shadow and claim the name you have given me as a small distinction, but I did not do this crime as I agree it is beneath us. Liseron."

Lupin knew not what to make of this. Does he believe this charlatan? The public seemed torn between either supporting each of them, disbelieving both of them, or thinking that Liseron was simply Lupin himself playing a game. And was there now a third "master criminal?"

Lupin pondered this as he stood on top of the Perret tower in Grenoble, examining the rubber ball which he had liberated from the police storage facility. He was tracing its manufacturers. But if he dropped it off this tower, what would the consequences be?

Q: *If Lupin dropped the rubber ball, and each time it bounced it reached half its original height, how many times would it bounce before it stopped?*

The Tides of Binic

I T WAS A CLEAR but cold February in 1903. The small port town of Binic was particularly beautiful at this time of day, but it was also strangely empty. Where normally dozens of boats and ships might jostle for space, today there were only four boats in the water. The usual people of the town were also absent for some reason, and a passing Lupin was very curious about this and wondered how he could turn it to his advantage.

The answer, apparently, was that the port was being used to test a new experimental military boat, named Aigrette. Lupin abandoned thoughts of exploiting the town's emptiness and instead watched with interest from his clear vantage point as the boat moved around the water with the three other vessels (a yacht, a small warship and a fishing vessel) being used for support and sometimes target practice.

Lupin admired how carefully the new boat's surface had been sealed to protect against any leaks. Sometimes Lupin couldn't see the new boat but was aware of its actions from the movement of the other ships. As he continued to watch he noted that the tide was coming in, and by 7:30 pm it would have reached its highest point of 12.91 m (42 ft).

Lupin noted that there was a small observation hut on the shore, and now that the tide was higher all three of the ships were level with the hut at their highest point. However, the fourth experimental ship was not, despite its height being exactly the same as the fishing vessel.

Q: *Why does the experimental ship's height not reach the same point as the fishing vessel's, despite the higher tide?*

The Disappearing Friend

LUPIN HAD SPENT A rather large percentage of his life either breaking into or escaping from places, and I wondered if there were any types of escape he had found difficult.

"I've had trouble with air escapes," he confessed. "When you are in a plane, being able to get away has a lot of obvious and dangerous complications! It's a rather modern problem but it does come up occasionally. And the answer is invariably a parachute."

He leaned in conspiratorially. "I was very nervous of using parachutes at first. An ally of mine told me that he and a friend had been stationed on an observation balloon in World War I. If the balloon was spotted, it was their policy to descend by parachute before the balloon was destroyed.

"However, as they jumped and activated their parachutes, his friend was blown massively off course by a sudden burst of wind! They went in opposite directions, miles apart, and he said that upon landing his friend had become tangled in a tree and broke his neck! He told me he never saw or heard about his friend again from the moment that they had jumped, a regret that lasted to that day."

Lupin now sat back. "Of course, later I realized his story could not be true, at least not entirely."

Q: *Why could Lupin's friend's story not be entirely true?*

The Strange Creature

SOMETIMES IN HIS EARLY days Lupin would not always know in advance exactly what he would be stealing. This would either be from crimes of opportunity, or simply because the horde or treasure he sought was described only in vague terms in history books or other sources.

One time he and a friend, a rather mischievous young Englishman named Stephen Travere, were breaking into a long-abandoned ceramics factory that in the past had been France's premier choice for kitchenware. They were concerned it had been taken over by dangerous wild animals, and intended to get the loot as quickly as possible. They found a locked room, but the door was impregnable, so they instead knocked a hole in a crumbling wall and Stephen peered through.

"Wait, I see something!" he said breathlessly. "It has a mouth!"

"An animal?!" Lupin asked frantically.

"I can see a neck and a lip . . ." Travere continued.

"Does it see you?" Lupin asked with concern.

"I can also see a face, but it can't see me. It looks rather flat and lifeless. I can also see, if you pardon my language, that it has a bottom."

"Do we need to go? Does it look strong?" asked Lupin, now somewhat confused.

"Quite strong, I think. It definitely has bones in it," Travere said, now with a smile creeping onto his face. "But they've probably been crushed. It looks like it can carry a lot of fluid weight but doesn't have it right now. I could grab it with one hand! Then perhaps we can have a drink together."

Lupin, realizing the joke, gave Travere a playful shove of annoyance.

Q: What can Travere see through the hole?

The Diabolical Door Code

ONE OF LUPIN'S RIVALS, the sinister Fantômas, wanted a meeting of criminals to carve up into dominions of France, as it were, and unsurprisingly few of the other criminals in the business wanted to go, as all it would take was a single leak for the event to be swooped upon by the Paris police, and they trusted Fantômas even less.

Fantômas managed to get many to attend through four statements: he challenged their bravado, he promised that the greatest chef in France would do the catering, he hired the most ruthless gang in Paris to cover security, and he devised a clever door code.

Lupin decided to attend—but disguised as another less prominent thief—and as he went to enter the hall, was surprised to see himself ahead of him in the queue! At first he thought it another criminal, but the way the man stood screamed "police officer" like the victim of a street robbery.

As the people entered, the doorman said a number and they replied.

"Six," said the doorman to Alfonse Duquette.

"Three," he replied and was admitted.

"Twelve," said the doorman to the man known as "The Tiger-skin Glove."

"Six," he replied, and he was admitted.

The fake Lupin smiled, and when the doorman said "Eight," he quickly replied "Four!" At this point security descended and began pummelling him, and it was only through jumping through a window he was able to escape. The real Lupin shook his head.

Q: How did the fake Lupin get it wrong?
What number should he have said?

The Riddle of the Clock

I N 1899 LOUIS LÉPINE became, for the second time, Préfet de Police in
Paris. However, his second time in the job, while successful in many
ways, would be dogged by the rising profile of Lupin, especially as the
national newspapers loved to print headlines such as "Lépine vs. Lupin?"
Achievements like his introduction of forensic methodology to police
work always felt like they were overshadowed by his inability to catch
Lupin.

Lupin himself tended to move between amusement at his inter-
actions with "The Little Man with the Big Stick" and annoyance that
people would think Lépine anywhere near being his match. Hence his
frustration when, in 1908, Lépine's men managed to catch Lupin and an
accomplice in the process of robbing the Monnaie de Paris. After Lupin
had escaped from jail and broken out his accomplice, he questioned how
it was possible they had known! Had Lépine somehow predicted his
actions?

No. As it turned out it was sheer luck on their part, Lépine accidentally ordering his men to go to the Monnaie instead of the house of
Manet, the painter, which is where he thought an actual robbery would
occur.

"Ah well, even a stopped clock is right twice a day," said Lupin's
accomplice.

"Actually, my friend, there is a town in Canada where this year, a
stopped clock will be right three times a day . . ."

"Impossible!"

"It's not! As they would say in Canada, 'I would bet the farm on it.'
But I'll save you the trouble of explaining how . . ."

Q: How is it possible for a stopped clock to be right three times a day?

The Falling Key

I N 1907 LUPIN FOUND himself imprisoned, not in France but in Ruritania, a country facing considerable political turmoil. For this reason, he had been betrayed by almost all of his supposed allies in the country so they could survive the ever-shifting political landscape, and now he was trapped in a tiny damp cell in the castle of Zenda, with some puffed-up member of their military gloating at him through the bars.

"I fancy you've been to this castle before, thief!" the general said, spitting the last word, "plotting your crime, crawling around! But I dare say you like this room much less!"

Lupin peered around. Decaying stone walls, no windows, no seat or bed, a bucket for ablutions and the constant drip of water on his head from a grille above.

"It has its charms," he said icily, somehow making the filthy rags they had forced him to wear seem as casual as a smoking jacket.

"Like this impenetrable iron door?" said the general, kicking it with his foot. "Three layers of super-hardened metal made right in this country. Just like the thick solid bricks around you, completely unbreakable. You're never getting out of here, fool."

"Not unless I had the key," said Lupin, slicking back his soaking wet hair.

"We've searched you very thoroughly," leered the general, "and you have no compatriots. So don't pretend to me you have any way of leaving this room."

"Perhaps not if it had been as cloudy as it was yesterday. But today the sun was out," Lupin said cryptically.

"Spare me your secret codes!" the general ranted. "I am not on your side—no one is! And you will never have . . ."

Lupin held his palm out flat and a key dropped directly into the middle of it.

". . . the key??" finished the general with confusion, and before he could utter another word Lupin had thrust the key into the lock and opened the very heavy metal door, slamming it directly into the general's torso. When he had recovered his breath Lupin was gone and it was the general who was locked in the cell, lying in a big puddle of water . . .

Q: *How did Lupin get the key without anyone helping him?*

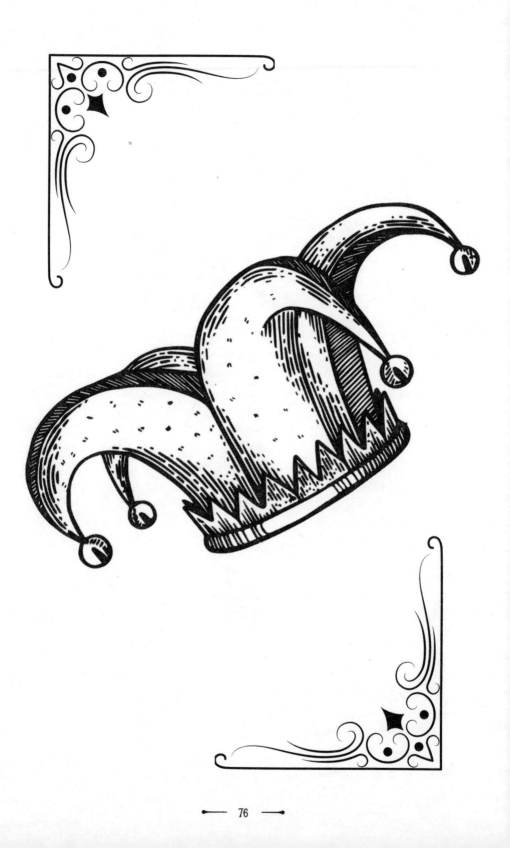

The Caught Jester

"EXPLAIN IT TO ME," said Louis Lépine. "Lupin was witnessed, dressed normally, entering the house through the front door at 3:15 am by a neighbour. The occupants are in their other house in Germany. At first the neighbour thought Lupin might be the owner as he has a similar build. Twenty minutes later he heard a muffled blast, the sound of metal falling and a brief shout, and then Lupin exited the house at 4:25 am . . . dressed as a jester."

Lépine shook his head at this detail, as he had before. "A jester? Do we know why?"

"No, sir. Claude thought that perhaps a circus might be nearby, and he meant to hide within it. But we checked and there was no circus."

"Hmm . . . Perhaps a play, at this nearby theatre?"

"At 4 in the morning, sir? There were no plays featuring jesters anyway, sir, even if he had hoped to wait for one to begin. The occupant of the house is a famous actor—remember that production of *King Lear* last year? But as you know, he is in Germany."

"Was there some advantage within the house to being dressed as a jester? Did they have a dog that was . . . afraid of jesters?" asked Lépine with slight desperation.

"No, sir, there was nothing there to steal. Their possessions had all been moved to Germany, almost all of their clothes, jewels, everything. Nothing left but a few mementos and a safe full of business papers, useless to most."

"But not to Lupin . . ." muttered Lépine.

"When we looked inside, we found only that the safe had been detonated with dynamite, a little too much, perhaps. We did find some burned scraps of cloth underneath a bare mannequin, but we don't know their significance . . ."

"THEN WHY A JESTER?!" shouted Lépine. "To mock me, to say I am a fool??"

"Sir . . . maybe the jester costume means nothing?"

And in a way the lieutenant was correct, but would never know why.

Q: Why was Lupin dressed as a jester?

The Honesty of Henri

LUPIN ALWAYS PREFERRED TO work alone, but he had a few valued allies. One of them, Henri Dargaud, was an unusual person even by Lupin's standards, in that despite being a skilled career criminal, he would always tell the truth. On her death bed, his mother, hoping to keep him from the dark path his father had trod, made him promise to never lie again. Instead of giving up crime, however, he simply found ways to avoid having to answer direct questions, and also trained his skills so that he was very rarely caught. There was the occasional infuriating time when he had to answer direct questions from the police and ended up in jail or incriminating someone else, so he had few friends beyond Lupin, but he kept to his word.

Another criminal, a thug named Pitof, hated Henri's honesty and kept trying to make him lie, but could never succeed. Then one day his friends grabbed Henri from behind and Pitof flipped a coin, hiding the result under his hand.

"Tell me, Henri, is it head or tails?"

Henri went to speak but Pitof held up a knife.

"And do not say you do not know! Say one word. You have half a chance to tell the truth!" Pitof said, laughing. "Is it head or tails?"

Henri considered this, and then gave a response he knew guaranteed he was telling the truth.

Q: *What one-word response did Henri give?*

The Cardinal Directions

LUPIN PREFERRED TO KNOW where he was going whenever he hid in small boats. When he had hidden in this boat it *had* been in the river Somme, but they started transporting it while he accidentally fell asleep.

Lupin knew that there were four possible destinations for this boat: north was Doullens, east was Assevillers, south was Crèvecœur-le-Grand, and west was Blangy-sur-Bresle. He needed to know which, as while Blangy and Crèvecœur-le-Grand had ways by which he could easily slip away, Doullens and Assevillers did not.

However, inside the hold he could not see where they were going. Occasionally he heard the voices of the drivers, but they did not show interest in discussing their destination, preferring instead an endless litany of the vices of their friends and family. Lupin couldn't sense their direction of travel either.

He tried searching amongst the objects on the boat; perhaps there would be a compass or something he could use to make one, or at least some kind of clue of its destination, but nothing. It was difficult enough to search without light, especially when the natural light coming through the slats at the helm of the boat began to dim and turn orange as the sun set.

Suddenly Lupin realized that the answer was as simple as night and day, and they were headed to Blangy-sur-Bresle.

Q: How did Lupin know their destination?

The Insurmountable Number

⸻•⸻

I T WAS AN EXTREMELY small combination lock, one whose numbers could only be seen with a magnifying glass and turned with the tip of a needle. Nonetheless it was also extremely strong, and if the combination was not entered correctly, then another needle, this one contained within the lock, would inject a quick-acting poison into Lupin's ankle, because that is where the lock was attached!

It was another gift from the Countess of Cagliostro, attached to him by an unseen assailant while he was distracted in the street. The same assailant must have been an extremely skilled pickpocket because he had also slipped a piece of paper into Lupin's jacket, on which was a 14-digit number and a riddle that presumably held the answer to the lock's combination, which had only 6 digits . . .

$$9\ 4\ 6\ 2\ 1\ 4\ 8\ 0\ 2\ 1\ 4\ 6\ 2\ 7$$

"The head and tail come first.
Other numbers are not even relevant,
unless they are the same when you stand on your head.
Then the last two are strangely the same."

Lupin had to think very quickly and act even quicker, but the combination of fear and excitement helped him decipher the riddle's meaning, and he was able to remove the deadly anklet just as the needle popped out!

Q: *What is the six-digit code that opened the lock?*

The Eggs of Fabergé

L UPIN WAS NOT A particular admirer of Fabergé eggs, beyond their
monetary value and the challenge of stealing them. He found their
design interesting but not aesthetically pleasing. So, when he managed
to secure some of the famous imperial eggs, he decided to reward his two
collaborators, especially considering the difficulty it took to break into
the Russian vaults to steal them.

The number of eggs he had couldn't be split equally, so he suggested
he didn't mind taking a smaller share as long as what they took was the
same amount.

Unfortunately, the first collaborator took this to mean that they
would take the same fraction of eggs, not the same quantity. So, he took
half the eggs and half of one Fabergé egg. The second collaborator then
also took half the remaining eggs and half of one egg, annoyed but still
happy to be getting a share of the loot. Lupin then took the remaining
single egg.

When he told me this, I was surprised that either of them would
accept half an egg, since its value would be considerably less, but he
simply smiled and said that no one walked away with an incomplete egg.

Q: How many Fabergé eggs were there to be divided up?

The Descenso del Diablo

LUPIN WAS OFTEN HAVING to climb up or down cliffs, castle walls, old, abandoned wells and on one occasion the side of a giant stone statue of Zeus. For this reason, he found it necessary to keep his climbing skills finely honed, often travelling to the Pas de la Casa in the Pyrenees to practise climbing on the steep mountain sides.

One particular cliff that he was determined to rappel down was the notorious Descenso del Diablo, a 55 m high sheer rock face. For efficiency's sake he only wanted to bring exactly as much rope as he would need to climb down. He knew that he could only drop 3 m without getting hurt, so would have to be extremely careful as he descended.

Furthermore, there were three sharp outcrops that could cause tension or wear on the rope, so he would need an extra 2 m of rope for each of those.

He also kept in mind that he was 1.79 m tall, and his arms were 65 cm from shoulder to wrist.

Q: *With all these considerations, what length of rope would Lupin need to successfully descend the cliff?*

The Ballad of Poor Jean

LUPIN PRIMARILY ROBBED THE rich, due to his moral code and because they had the nicest things. Therefore, when Lupin told me he intended to rob an old man in Butte-Chaumont, an area of Paris riddled with poverty, I was confused.

Jean Charbonneau lived in a tiny run-down apartment just like his neighbours, in cramped conditions, especially as there was one room of his residence he refused to enter. Why would the great Arsène Lupin rob such a wretched soul? He gave me no answer as we entered the building, only that I would see.

The apartment looked to me as threadbare and penurious as the rest. His bed's springs were bent and broken. "From Monsieur Charbonneau's prodigious weight . . ." is all Lupin had to say.

Charbonneau had a single pair of simple shoes. Lupin held them up to his face, covering his eyes. "Perhaps he does not even wear these, otherwise why no holes?" he said.

We moved through to the small kitchen and Lupin picked up a small hat nearby.

"Vicuna wool. Perhaps he has been to the Andes, where these rare creatures live. But not big enough to keep his head warm, poor Jean," he said, feeling the fabric.

Lupin knocked on the wall, testing its integrity and finding it quite hollow-sounding, although somewhere in the building I heard what seemed like a cascade of metal.

He then moved past a bowl of black eggs to a dusty-looking bottle of wine with the label half hanging off. As he lifted it, the label fell and I briefly glanced "1846 Meursault Charmes" before he casually placed it on the table. "Poor fellow can only afford very old wine." Then Lupin revealed what was hidden underneath, a single gold sovereign.

"He tells everyone in the neighbourhood this is his only valuable possession, a gift from a famous general," he said, pocketing the coin.

"And you would steal it?!" I exclaimed, horrified.

"Yes, I will. This is no hiding spot. It was merely misplaced. And then perhaps I will talk to M. Charbonneau about the importance of generosity . . ."

Q: Why does Lupin feel happy stealing this man's gold coin?

The History of L'histoire de Cardenio

F OR CENTURIES PEOPLE HAVE sought William Shakespeare's famous lost manuscripts, and one of those was *The History of Cardenio*, a play known to have been performed by Shakespeare's acting company The King's Men in 1613.

Many forgeries had been "discovered" over the years, so when the rich businessman Antoine Bonheur was approached by an archivist who claimed to have found an original copy in the catacombs of London, he was naturally dubious.

"It seemed like an obvious fraud," Antoine said to his friend Luis, "but the man permitted me to submit the manuscript to several experts, both in Shakespeare and in old documents, and they said that it passes all their tests! Can you imagine the publicity when I reveal I have *L'histoire de Cardenio*?"

"It's in French?" said Luis, raising an eyebrow.

"Oh yes, Shakespeare's plays were often translated. This is perhaps less valuable than the English original, but still incredible!"

"What happens in the play?" asked Luis.

Antoine waved his hand in a dismissive way that Luis knew meant he had not read it properly. "Oh, it's remarkable. Cardenio falls in love with Luscinia, he travels the world to pursue her, he scales the Great Wall of China, there's a scene at the Taj Mahal where they ride elephants."

Antoine looked at the notes he had been given.

"There's a comic scene with a barometer that only tells the wrong weather, and then a scene where a barber and a priest get drunk on sparkling champagne and bottled beer, and keep losing important objects by flushing them down the toilet . . . There's even a clever scene where Cardenio finds the First Folio of Shakespeare's other plays and mocks them!"

Luis held up his hand.

"My friend, this is a scam. I do not know who the experts you employed were, but they too are in on the game. Perhaps you were influenced to select them by the so-called archivist . . ."

That's how *I* would do it, thought Lupin, as that is who Luis was.

"No . . . perhaps," said Antoine, "but how do you know it's not genuine?"

"As a . . . connoisseur of antiquity, I have acquired a certain level of historical knowledge. And five things you have told me indicate this manuscript must have been written after Shakespeare's death."

Q: What are the five anachronistic details that show the manuscript was written after 1616 (when Shakespeare died)?

The Truffle Pig

T HE USE OF PIGS to find truffles has gone on for centuries, and in 1906 resulted in the first ever *famous* truffle pig, Madame Veritas.

The smallest in her litter, she eventually showed an aptitude for truffle finding that left her sisters in the shade. Her owner was a farmer who leased land from the Marquis of Landreville, and he generously "decided" to donate her to the Marquis. After that her local celebrity grew to a national sensation, due to her distinctive heart-shaped skin marking.

The Marquis had a special pigsty built so that the public could come and see her for a small fee, and it was very popular, especially with children. His social rival, The Duke of Danon, tried to compete by buying a prize boar named Bucephalus, but no one seemed interested.

It was from her special pigsty that Madame Veritas was stolen one April night, and of course Lupin was suspected. As the thief could clearly not capitalize on her fame, everyone assumed Lupin wanted the pig for its amazing truffle-finding skills, and a country-wide search commenced.

Lupin had no interest in stealing pigs, not this year anyway, so he sent a message to the newspapers declaring this and suggesting they think about the children.

For some reason this led the public and police to start suspecting a group of Romani who were encamped in the area, and they were rounded up and arrested as a group. Lupin then sent a subsequent, angrier letter, suggesting that if they didn't release the Romani and start thinking more clearly, he would personally steal the stained glass pig from the Chapelle Notre-Dame-de-Lhor in Moselle, "where many had been christened."

Then, almost 120 days after she was taken, Madame Veritas was returned, seeming a little tired and thinner, but otherwise no worse for wear. No one seemed to have the answer to the mystery, and Lupin's only final message to the press was to "check the Marquis's litter." The police looked through his trashcans but found nothing.

Q: *Why was Madame Veritas pignapped?*

The Fateful Date of Robespierre

A NOTHER TIME I WORKED with Lupin, he asked me to come over to France from London in disguise on this fishing trawler. I swear I was on that boat for two days before I realized Lupin was the captain.

"What is it this time—Napoleon's undergarments?" I asked, grumpy that he'd been having me haul fishnets for three hours.

"Actually, this is an artefact once owned by a Monsieur Maximilien Robespierre. An ornate calendar, a memento of the revolution."

I didn't know much about the revolution, but I told Lupin I knew Robespierre was considered either a bloody saint or a right rotter by the French.

"Some say he was both at once," Lupin mused. "In fact, it can be said that he was executed both on the 28th day of the seventh month, but also on the 10th day of the eleventh month."

"Are you talking about 10 Thermidor in the Second Year of Freedom?" said a passing sailor, who evidently was not a real fisherman either.

"Yes, about 74 past 5 on the day of the watering can!" replied Lupin, and they both laughed. Lupin revealed that on the 21st September 1792 the revolutionaries brought in a whole new calendar, decimalized with 12 new months, with 30 days a month and 10 days a week! By our calendar, the year started on the 22nd of September in Vendémiaire and ended on the 16th of the following September in Fructidor, with five complimentary national holiday days in between. The months were:

- Autumn—Vendémiaire, Brumaire and Frimaire.

- Winter—Nivôse, Pluviôse and Ventôse.

- Spring—Germinal, Floréal and Prairial.

- Summer—Messidor, Thermidor and Fructidor.

"So if my birthday is the 30th of August, what date would that be in the French Republican calendar?" said Lupin cheekily. "I'll give you a decimal minute to guess. That's 86 seconds in normal time . . ."

Q: What date and month in the French Republican calendar is the 30th of August?

Sylvie's Beloved

LUPIN KNEW THAT THE final piece of the D'Argent bracelet must have been given to Robert d'Argent's daughter, Sylvie. Having found the first two pieces in the burial places of her cousins, he fully expected the final part to have been buried with her.

However, he knew that Sylvie's beliefs were even more radical than her Egypt-obsessed cousin, Quentin. Sylvie fancied herself a poetic druidess who loved nature and animals and wanted to be part of it, so when she died, she had been burned on a funeral pyre of green wood, and her ashes had been scattered to the winds.

"It would have been more natural if they had buried her—at least the worms could have feasted," thought Lupin as he leafed through old documents. All he could find was that her "greatest treasure was buried with her beloved," but she never married and there was no record of any relationships or affairs.

Eventually he found his answer in a poem that Sylvie had written, although it pointed to a larger mystery. The poem filled almost an entire volume and was extremely dull and florid, but Lupin managed to extract some key pieces of information about her "beloved."

- Their relationship was chaste but passionate.
- He had very long flowing grey hair, but was quite young.
- He had a long, noble nose.
- He was strong and muscular, and was known for his ability to run fast.
- In his youth he ran wild, but she tamed him.

When Lupin read that he only ate vegetables, he thought that was very unusual for the time, until he suddenly realized who her beloved was, and felt very foolish. It was definitely unusual for those like her beloved to have marked graves, but he found it, and retrieved the final part of the Medici bracelet soon after.

Q: *Why is it unusual that her beloved had a marked grave?*

The Fall of Marianne

L UPIN WAS FALLING AT high speed toward the Mediterranean, his arms tucked close to his body. The reason was simple but frustrating.

Lupin had been carefully planning the robbery of some priceless jewels in St-Jean-Cap-Ferrat, targeting the house of the rich widow Simone de Rochefort. During this time, he became aware that she was being targeted by another robber, a less careful, ungentlemanly fellow known as Edgard.

Lupin considered a scheme to send Edgard off elsewhere, but instead decided it was better to meet with him and agree that they would collaborate on robbing the Villa Maximillian and split the profits.

Edgard had seemed very amenable to the arrangement and the robbery had gone smoothly, up until the point at which they were to escape by rappelling down from the Villa's huge balcony to a waiting speedboat in the Med. At this point, Edgard apparently decided that Lupin would remain as a scapegoat, and grabbed him, attempting to knock him out.

The two struggled and knocked into a precarious statue of Marianne (personification of the Republic) that stood on the balcony's edge. The statue smashed the railing and Edgard attempted to throw Lupin off into the sea, to fall 30 m (98 ft) and break all his bones on its surface! Lupin resisted, and ironically it was Edgard himself who fell, followed seconds later by the statue of Marianne, and then Lupin, too unbalanced to stop!

Edgard hit the surface on his back with his arms splayed out, and suffered multiple fractures and contusions. He remains in the hospital there to this day. The statue hit the water and then, twisting his body so his feet were toward the water, Lupin hit the water seconds later.

However, despite multiple sprains and bruises, Lupin was able to climb into the speedboat and even help drag the unconscious and injured Edgard into the boat as well.

"Thank the lord for Marianne!" said the boat's driver.

"I did not need her help," said Lupin.

Q: *How did Lupin avoid being injured as badly as Edgard?*

The Cheese Vaults of Bassoues

ONCE THE VAULTS UNDER the Chateau de Bassoues held the tombs of the many ancestors of those who lived within the castle. But since it had been bought by the rich cheese exporter Gaston DeGarmo, the ancestors had been rather disrespectfully moved to the town's graveyard and the vaults were now used for the storage of many different types of cheese from all over the country.

However, some found it more disrespectful of DeGarmo to store all the different types of cheeses together than they did that he had thrown out the corpses of the castle's long-ago occupants! The locals loved all cheeses, from the blue veins of Roquefort to the powerfully odiferous Camembert, and Comté's hard texture and slightly sweet taste. They said they would even eat the holes of a wheel of Emmenthal!

Lupin did not particularly care either way. His main aim was to find his way out. He had planned this to be his exit route from the castle after taking a few valuable jewels, but despite having mapped it, he found himself lost in the labyrinth of curdled milk that lay around him. None of the cheese was marked, possibly from carelessness, but he knew that he had to go through the Camembert, then the Roquefort, then finally the Emmenthal. There was also some Reblochon and Comté down here.

The first crossroads he came to had two possible directions, left and right. On the left the cheeses were an orangey-yellow colour. He tried a piece and found it was slightly nutty. On the right the cheeses had a white rind and a very pungent smell! He chose his direction.

The next crossroads had three exits: more of the pungent cheese to his left, some blue veined cheese with a crumbly texture ahead, and a yellowy cheese with many holes to his right. He chose his direction again.

Finally, there were two last directions. On the left more of the yellowy cheese with holes, and on the right a very solid-looking cheese with a dark brown rind. He chose and escaped.

Q: Which direction did he choose at the first, second and third crossroads?

The Villainous Vineyard

LUPIN MOVED SLOWLY BETWEEN the vines. The ground was steep and the sunlight strong, so he had to watch his footing and keep low to ensure he could not be seen.

He suspected this was the vineyard from which the poisoned champagne was sent. Figures across France had been taken gravely ill after drinking champagne.

The bottles had different labels, locations and vintages, but after a close encounter with a bottle of it himself, Lupin had investigated and found that the poison must have been added at the source.

He followed the supply lines to here, and had seen various hooded figures moving in and out of the main buildings. Under their dark red robes hid pale white faces. They looked like cultists. He could not yet understand what their aim was, but Lupin knew he would put an end to it right now.

But wait . . . for a second Lupin suddenly noticed the grapes that surrounded him were red! Pinot Noir grapes, unless he was mistaken! As he looked along the rows and then across the entire vineyard, he saw that all the grapes were red! How could the champagne have come from here? Perhaps he was in the wrong place?

But then he stopped and thought, noting that a nearby press was designed to operate very gently. He shook his head. The sun had clearly got to him. This was definitely the right place.

Q: *How can this be the place the champagne came from?*

The Tiflis Raid

W HEN I MET LUPIN in 1932, he was ruefully remembering the notorious bank raid in Tiflis in 1907.

"A stagecoach was transporting money through Erivansky Square, in what was then called the Russian Empire," he said. "A group attacked with bombs, 40 people died and 50 more were injured."

"And they suspected you?"

"Yes! The only thing I never steal is a man's life, and yet so many of these violent crimes are laid at my feet. The authorities suspected it was masterminded by a man named Kamo, a supposed master of disguise who once cut a heart from a man's chest! And they thought I was he."

"So, what happened?"

"They captured the real Kamo, and after years of feigning madness, escape and capture, they gave him four death sentences."

"And he was executed?"

"No. In fact ten years after the robbery they just . . . let him go. After the Russian Revolution he had friends in high places."

I was confused. "And the other robbers, did they receive punishment?"

Lupin's eyes twinkled, "Not exactly. One of them, Vladimir Ilyich Ulyanov, had Erivansky Square named after him in 1921! They named a lot of places after him, actually. Saint Petersburg, for one! And another of them, Joseph "Koba the Great," has a very high position in government right now."

I was horrified. How was this possible?

Q: *Why was Kamo released, and who were the two other robbers?*

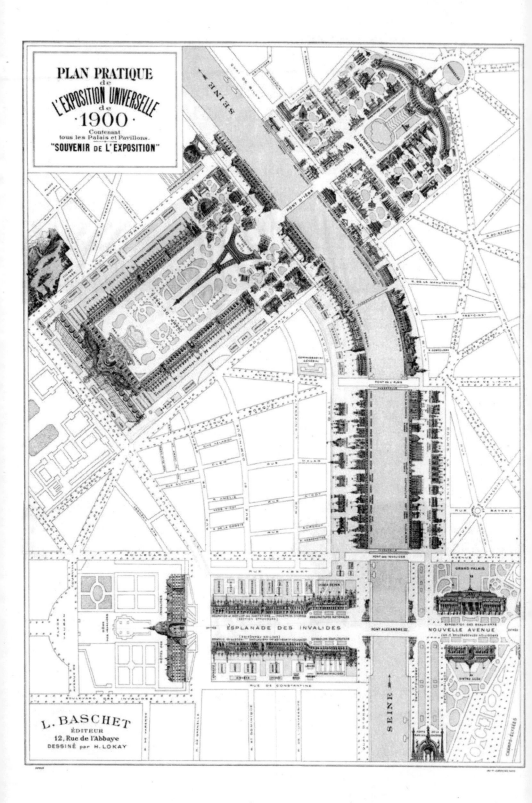

Paris Exposition

THE PARIS EXPOSITION OF 1900 was an enormous cultural event, a festival of innovation and a celebration of art and technology that showed the very best that Paris and France had to offer as it entered the new century.

Lupin felt like the art of crime and the technology of sophisticated theft deserved recognition too, but he had drawn a line at trying to have a pavilion at the exhibition. Instead, he had decided to represent his field by stealing parts of the Exposition after it had been dismantled.

However, he had underestimated the ant-like diligence of the Exposition's workers and having waited a year for his opportunity, found that it was being taken to pieces at a lightning rate, and its treasures being taken far and wide in dozens of different trains and carts! Even with his intel, he struggled to keep abreast of whether a train contained items from one of the 40 different international pavilions like China or Russia, the Grand Palais with its many paintings, the Palace of Optics with its giant kaleidoscopic hall of mirrors, or the Petit Palais, or the other palaces or . . . There were many possibilities.

In the end Lupin simply decided to choose a particular train at random, and the contents would be his. Fate would decide whether that was a pile of jewel-studded chandeliers or just some panels of broken wood.

He easily snuck onto the train, and as it dashed through the countryside he found the transportation carriage and, throwing open the doors, was suddenly confronted by a baffling sight: dozens of other Lupins! He threw up his arms and they threw up their arms too. Among them lay strange, curved structures, like bones, and small statues. Smiling, Lupin waved at them with his left hand, and they waved back with their right. He closed the doors and reflected on how he would profit from this . . .

Q: *What did Lupin find in the carriage?*

The Time of Release

WHEN IN PRISON, LUPIN'S wildly bearded cellmate was annoyed that Lupin seemed disinterested in his plan to steal the Great Wall of China, and had taken to planning his own escape.

"I have watched the guards carefully," he told Lupin, "and I have noticed there is a moment every day when none of them are paying attention."

"When is that?" asked Lupin.

"When I am asleep," he said. "They are always watching me when I am awake, so logically it makes sense that when I sleep they see nothing!"

Lupin decided not to comment.

"So, all I need to do is escape while I am still asleep! My brother used to sleepwalk when we lived together as children, so as long as I dream that I am my own brother, I can escape this place!"

Lupin considered this.

"But aren't you supposed to be released soon?"

The bearded man cackled. "Soon? Not at all. The month before two months after the month before next month is July, and that is when I am due for release!"

Q: How long does the man have before he is released?

The Barrel of Napoleon

LUPIN PREFERRED NOT TO drink alcohol, for reasons that he designated "hygiene," though he would explain no further. This meant that the occasions when he stole valuable wines or spirits gave him less pleasure than when he took a beautiful painting or an ornate piece of jewellery.

Nonetheless, when the opportunity came to get his hands on a barrel of Napoleon's personal reserve of Cognac, Lupin did not waste any time. In the past he had compared himself to the former emperor (with a sense of irony), so he felt a strange attraction to any artefacts left from his life.

As he rolled the barrel up from the cellar, Lupin suddenly stopped and turned around to his cohort, Grognard. He opened the lid and peered inside.

"Level with me, have you had a taste of the contents? I do not blame you if that is the case, I simply wish to know how much to deduct from your share of the money . . ." Lupin said playfully.

Grognard shook his head. "No, sir."

"The reason I ask is that when I first inspected this it was more than half-full, and now I suspect it is slightly less than half," he continued.

They both peered inside.

"It looks the same to me, sir," Grognard said. "We must move quickly, there's no time to weigh or measure it . . ."

"I don't need to," said Lupin, smiling. "I have a little tip on how to tell if it's more than half full or more than half empty."

Q: *How can he tell if it's more than half full or half empty without measuring the liquid or removing any?*

The Mysterious Meal

ONE TIME LUPIN SAT with four other thieves at the end of a fine meal. They could not decide how to share the cost, each alternately either trying to be generous or claiming poverty in their playful way. In the end Lupin suggested a strange compromise.

"The person who has eaten the creature with the smallest number of feet will pay," he declared.

"Well, I had the steak, and cows have four feet," said one.

"Ah, but I had chicken, and they have two feet, so I think I may be in the lead. You are out of it entirely, I think, Jean, you had the crab, and they have 10 legs!"

"Yes, but they have no feet!" said Jean. "However, I did also have some wild boar, and they have four."

"Gentlemen, I have tricked you," Lupin confessed. "I never eat meat and therefore I must pay for everything."

"I am delighted to hear that," said Alphonse, pushing his plate of empty shells to the side, "as the animal I ate has but one foot, and I thought it would be me who paid."

The group were confused—what animal has only one foot? "Did it lose a foot in a fight?"

"No, it was born with only one, as are all its kind," Alphonse said, wiping garlic butter from his mouth.

Q: What animal naturally has only one foot?

The Unwanted Delivery

I N 1924, FRANCE WAS abuzz with the news that the famed factory owner Emile Blanchet had been found to possess *Baptism* by Nicolas Poussin, a painting that had been stolen 12 years previously. Blanchet admitted that he had received it and hung it in a secret antechamber in his mansion, but claimed that he had personally hired Arsène Lupin to steal it for him from his previous German owner as an act of patriotism.

Lupin was enraged by this as he sat with me and his long-suffering ally Grognard inside a small bistro they preferred.

"I have never stolen anything on commission! I am not a common deliveryman! I steal only for myself."

Grognard made a small dismissive noise. "Bof!"

"Do you have something to say?"

"I was just thinking of the time that Guy DeHeliot, the ivory trader, summoned us to his estate in Lyon. We walked past those endless cages, pens, hutches and sties, filled with all his acquisitions from abroad. He requested you steal something for him from Versailles, connected to the heraldry of his home. And two days later that very thing was right there in his bedroom!"

Lupin smiled. "I suppose you are right. However, DeHeliot was not very happy with the result, was he? He felt personally attacked by it. I thought it was a roaring success."

Q: What did Lupin steal for DeHeliot, and why was he not happy?

The Visiting Card

O N THE 14TH OF March 1921, Inspector Ganimard brushed the broken glass from his shoes, concerned he might track it into the house from the front lawn, and looked at the Duke's drawing room, which was missing many valuable items of furniture.

The Duke stood nearby, his face a mask of self-pity.

"I have only myself to blame, Monsieur. Lupin sends me his card to say he will rob me, and I do nothing—I assume my security is perfect. An arrogant fool!"

He pointed to his two primary guards, standing nearby rubbing sore arms and stretching their backs. They said they had both somehow missed the robbers. The Duke was angry at their incompetence but had sworn to keep them on as he knew their families.

Ganimard looked at the room, with the heavy drag marks across the wooden floor and several dents in the wall and door frames.

Then Ganimard looked at Lupin's card. As a Lupin expert, he could tell it was authentic.

"You have an interesting set of furniture in your drawing room, which I desire for myself." The card had a small but comprehensive list of everything that had been taken, then continued: "I shall pay you a visit on the night of the Ides and carefully, cleanly remove them, and it would give both of us the smallest amount of disruption if you arranged to be away on that day."

"You have insurance?" Ganimard asked.

"Of course, but monetary reimbursement cannot compensate for my feelings of deep personal loss," said the Duke. "You must find this Lupin, inspector! Find the fiend who cleared out my drawing room!"

"I think I have already found him," said Ganimard, tucking the card into his pocket. "I will have to ask you to accompany me."

Q: Why does Ganimard suspect the Duke?

The Bells of Notre Dame

I N VICTOR HUGO'S *The Hunchback of Notre Dame*, the titular character, Quasimodo, is deaf from his constant exposure to the incredibly loud bells of the cathedral in which he lived. But the real-life bellringers of Notre Dame could attest to the fact that even a singular exposure to the ringing of one of the bells could lead to deafness and agonizing pain, even causing a dangerous shock to those with weak hearts.

These were words Arsène Lupin ensured he remembered as he ascended the stairs to the top of the South Tower of Notre Dame de Paris, a slightly wriggling sack over his shoulder.

Lupin had been visiting a bird-trainer friend of his when he received a message to meet the reclusive master forger known only as Le Style, to learn why he had created such brilliant satirical forgeries, and whether he was aligned with the Lupin copycat who had now claimed the name Liseron.

Le Style wanted to meet directly next to the famous Emmanuel bell, cast in 1686 and beloved of all France. Lupin was anticipating some kind of trick or ambush, so had a surprising ally with him, and the method of summoning them in his pocket.

As he reached the top, he could see a shadowy figure standing next to a bell. The figure stepped into the light, and he saw an elderly but solidly built man with a military moustache and a fanatical glint in his eyes. He wore ear protectors.

"So, this is the famous master thief," said Le Style in an accent Lupin recognized.

"You are Russian?" Lupin said with surprise.

"Crimean," responded Le Style, bitterly, "and you are French, a country full of thieves. The bell I care about is not the Emmanuel, but this one," he touched the bell with affection, "the fog bell of Chersonesos, stolen from my hometown of Sevastopol during the war. This is a world of hypocrites and fools, and you are one of the worst, the bandit king of a corrupt nation. We are now enemies."

Le Style now revealed that he held a sledgehammer and went to slam it against the bell and possibly deafen them both. Thinking quickly, Lupin put his hand in his pocket and then rang a bell before Le Style could! Lupin's ally appeared in an instant and angrily flew at Le Style, allowing Lupin to escape.

Q: *Why did the bell Lupin rang not deafen him or his ally?*
They did not wear ear protectors and neither of them was deaf.

The Beheading Game

A STATUE OF LANCELOT, THE legendary knight and member of King Arthur's Round Table at Camelot, was erected in the town of Troyes, the supposed birthplace of Chrétien de Troyes. Chrétien was the author of many chivalric romance stories that popularized Lancelot, and the townsfolk felt a statue was not inappropriate.

What *was* inappropriate was that the statue had been commissioned by the mayor and sculpted, poorly, by his brother, and furthermore people noticed the statue bore rather a close resemblance to the mayor as well. People grumbled, but the mayor was powerful and vindictive, so there was nothing to be done.

Or so it seemed, because Arsène Lupin sent the mayor a message:

"Monsieur Mayor, in the classic tales Lancelot played a beheading game, cutting off an enemy's head only for the foe to reattach it and pledging to do the same to him. I give you one week to remove your statue, or I will come and take its head."

The mayor was not only powerful but proud. He would not remove the statue. He thought to post guards on it but knew Lupin would have a way to circumvent them. Any form of protection, whether fences, cages or spikes, would fail. He knew of only one way to ensure Lupin could not behead the statue.

One week later in the dead of night, Lupin arrived at the statue with tools and equipment, only to find that he was unable to fulfil his pledge. A Pyrrhic victory for the mayor, but a victory nonetheless . . .

Q: How did the mayor stop Lupin from beheading the statue?

The Revolutionary Cake

"**Y**OUR GUESTS ARE STARVING," said Arnon Belmont's head waiter. Belmont had intended to stage a miraculous banquet and fireworks show, but when inspecting the fireworks, Belmont had inadvertently set fire to his mansion's kitchen. The workers were safe, but all the food was ruined, save for the ceremonial gateau in the central hall. Belmont had then decided to drown his sorrows in wine.

"What was it Marie Antoinette said?" grumbled Belmont. "Let them eat cake!"

His head waiter raised an eyebrow. "Monsieur, there are 230 people, and the cake has but 12 slices."

"Irrelevant!" shouted Belmont. "Antoinette fed all the peasants with cake. I'm sure I can do the same!"

The head waiter rubbed his forehead. "Monsieur, I think you may be confused about the story. Even if Antoinette said, 'let them eat cake,' which is doubtful, she was not thinking of how much cake it would take. In 1789 there were 28 million people in France. Monsieur Berthelot the chemist proposes that a human being needs 2,000 calories every day to live, and a slice of cake has 250 calories, so can you imagine how many cakes it would take to feed all of France just for one day?"

Belmont drunkenly tried to imagine this, not realizing his "head waiter" was distracting him from the robbery he was masterminding . . .

Q: Can you calculate how many cakes it would take to feed all of France just for one day?

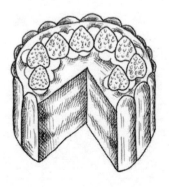

All for One

LUPIN HAD THOUGHT STEALING the draft manuscript of Dumas's novel *The Three Musketeers* would be an easy task. But he had not reckoned with the fact that The Dumas Club, the manuscript's current owners, were actually some sort of underground criminal organization in their own right, and not simply an informal group of enthusiasts.

As he hung upside down in their dungeon, Lupin had time to reflect on this, and was relieved when the club's de facto leader came down to speak to him.

"I trust that you see yourself as a musketeer, valiantly liberating the book from agents of the cardinal . . ." the man said. "But in truth you are more like Milady de Winter, duplicitous and amoral."

"Actually, I see myself more as Queen Anne . . ." said Lupin.

"So master thief, here's a riddle for you. Athos, Porthos, Aramis and D'Artagnan have their backs to a wall, fighting the cardinal's men. One of them has the Queen's diamonds in his coat pocket. Which? I can tell you this:

- "The diamonds are held by one who stands to the left of a musketeer with an A in his name.
- "The musketeer with the diamonds has neither the longest nor the shortest name.
- "The musketeer with the diamonds has a name ending in S.
- "The musketeer with the diamonds has a wine in their name."

Q: *Who has the Queen's diamonds—Athos, Porthos, Aramis or D'Artagnan?*

The Prisoner's Dilemma

T HE SECRETIVE NATION OF Borostyria became aware, through its spy network, that the dangerous foreign criminal Arsène Lupin was operating within its borders, with the help of another agent known only as "Mr. H." The spies reported that both men were able to stay under the radar due to their generic appearance and skill at disguise, as well as deliberately staying apart so they could not be caught simultaneously.

However, Lupin was unable to escape their regard for too long, and was captured and thrown into a dark cell in the notoriously grim dungeons of Barantis Castle, a bristling fortress of black stone with a poisonous moat and networks of tunnels underneath.

Lupin had no food, no water, no natural light and no human contact, save for when the guards did their daily check.

Soon afterward, Mr. H was captured as well and put in a cell on the other side of the dungeons, to ensure there would be no collusion between the two. He, too, was starved in total darkness with no contact.

"One of them will crack, that is certain, and betray the other in exchange for leniency," said the chief interrogator.

"I am not so sure," said the chancellor. "They are compatriots, they have acted in concert, they even look alike."

"That means they think alike. Which means they will both suspect that the other will confess and try to pre-empt each other!"

"I hope so. Ancient Borostyrian law does dictate that if after six days neither of them confesses, they must be released," said the chancellor. "I think they know this."

"One of them will crack."

However, they did not know that Lupin could be a hundred percent certain that Mr. H would not betray him, and six days later they were forced to release Lupin and then Mr. H without charge.

Q: *How could Lupin be sure that Mr. H would not betray him?*

The Eiffel Conundrum

A S SOON AS LUPIN became known as a skilled thief in France, there was one question that everyone was always asking: would he rob the Eiffel Tower? Newspapers dedicated whole pages to the question, shop owners and landowners alike would speculate on the possibility, and there was even a song released on the subject which sold remarkably well. Lupin himself stayed silent on the subject until 1924, when he released a statement saying:

"I have no comment on whether or not he plans to rob the Eiffel Tower next month. —Arsène Lupin."

No one was more flummoxed by this than the police. Surely he was lying, and this meant he would definitely rob it. And why specify next month? Did that mean he would rob it then, or next week, or next year? What if he knew they would think that? And what if he knew they knew he would think they thought that?

A week after that, Lupin released another statement:

"I regret if my previous statement was difficult to understand, and offer the following clarification: I would like to deny that I have no desire to consider not planning to undertake to refuse a confirmation that I may not decide not to rob the Eiffel Tower. —Arsène Lupin."

The police considered taking a short simultaneous vacation.

Q: Does Lupin's second statement mean he plans to rob the Eiffel Tower?

The Secret of the Apartment

ONCE THE POLICE HAD concluded that Lupin *would* rob the Eiffel Tower, their next quandary was: what is there to steal from the Eiffel Tower? Some money was kept in the restaurants, but this was considered to be below Lupin. Some suggested he might steal parts of its physical structure, like rivets or the top of the tower, and it was a testament to Lupin's legend that this was only dismissed by the more practically minded members of the police and public.

What the police decided was most likely was that Lupin would rob Gustave Eiffel's personal apartment, the small but well-appointed space at the top of the tower where he would entertain guests as illustrious as Thomas Edison. The police asked Eiffel if he had anything rare and very valuable in his apartment, and he answered truthfully that he did not.

This is because Lupin had actually robbed Eiffel's apartment several weeks before he had sent the messages!

Eiffel had, in fact, possessed in his apartment something he was not meant to have: a small model originally intended for one of his company's clients that had been "accidentally" lost. Eiffel had decided he wanted it for himself because he felt it was a good example of his structural design. It was rare and made from platinum rather than the copper from which the actual structure was constructed.

Lupin had gained access to the apartment in the guise of Guglielmo Marconi, the radio pioneer, knowing that Eiffel had never met him in person. While Eiffel went to procure more champagne, Lupin found the hiding spot of the item, instantly recognizable. The structure it represented was huge and had become an iconic symbol of the city it occupied, welcoming visitors from all over the globe!

Q: Of what structure was the item a model?

Lupin vs Gustave Eiffel

———————●———————

L UPIN SWIFTLY CONCEALED THE item when Eiffel re-entered the room, bearing not champagne but a loaded pistol.

"I think you will not enjoy the popping sound that *this* makes, Monsieur Lupin," said Eiffel. "I took the liberty of calling Monsieur Marconi's company and he is currently visiting Montpelier Observatory."

"It is *I* who will be taking the liberty, Monsieur Eiffel," said Lupin, seemingly unconcerned. "You are not supposed to have this model, and it would damage your reputation considerably if this became public."

"This is why you will pass it to me now, or we will be forced to test the effect of a body falling from the tower. This has been a concern of mine due to the fallibility of the elevators and the possibility of fire . . ."

"So, you have an alternative route of escape," said Lupin, looking around Eiffel's luxurious apartment at the many items of gold, velvet and, intriguingly, some folded silk.

"Yes, a man named Franz Reichelt had developed . . . enough talk! You are in over your head. Pass me the model now!" said Eiffel, his finger on the trigger. He was paranoid enough to shoot.

Lupin paused . . . and then instead threw a nearby model of the Eiffel Tower itself, its sharp point nearly skewering Eiffel as he leapt to the side.

Lupin had but a moment, so he grasped the thing he had earlier noticed, and with a few swift movements had escaped Eiffel's slow descent into madness, and minutes later was away from the tower itself with his prize.

Lupin had been seen during his escape, and Eiffel was forced to claim it was in fact a dummy to hide the events that had happened. However, I did suspect that when Lupin told me this tale, he may have been pulling my leg, or at least some strings . . .

Q: *How did Lupin escape from the Eiffel's apartment?*

The Riddle of the Fires

A PATRON OF AN ART gallery that Lupin was visiting (with an eye to returning later) was staring with disgust at one of the new modern paintings with its bold jagged lines and bright hues.

"How horrific!" she snorted, clutching her chest. "It is so primitive!"

Lupin feigned agreement. "But of course, Mademoiselle. But I had an even more bizarre and primitive encounter only last night!"

She turned to him, intrigued.

"I entered a room," he continued, "and inside were people clad in animal skin, some of them even covered in dried fluids extracted from worms! They were drinking the rancid juice of potatoes!"

"Mon Dieu!" the woman exclaimed.

"I could hear the banging of drums! I saw a man in front of me light a fire! No one remarked—in fact I suddenly saw they had all lit fires! The room was filled with smoke, but no one did anything!"

The woman began to show signs of feeling faint, and when she recovered she was surprised to find Lupin gone . . . as well as her diamond bracelet. She never realized what he had described was totally normal and something she had encountered many times . . .

Q: What had Lupin encountered?

Riddle of the Chimera

O NE OF LUPIN'S ASSOCIATES was a rogue zoologist named Bob "Saltie" Aberdeen. He provided information and occasionally biological samples so he could acquire money to pursue his true passion of thwarting poachers and unscrupulous hunters.

The thing he had most contempt for was other zoologists, who in his opinion were primarily dusty old men who rarely came into contact with the animals they studied, preferring to use second-hand reports and the occasional stuffed creature.

"When I was visiting the Zoological Society of London there was this right bunch of old fossils. I reckon most of them had already been around since Charlie Darwin was an office boy shining their shoes. They took against me because of my accent and because I put my dirty boots up on some 300-year-old table or something. Asked me to meet them in some viewing gallery and turned all the lights off, wanted to give me a scare with a stuffed leopard.

"Well I had a little pet of my own so I released it into the dark room and they went spare. Screaming and running around. I had to retrieve it in case the silly old fools trod on it by accident. One of them might have got a bit knocked out and I caught them later around his sick bed trying to figure it out."

"It was a snake, I am sure of it, the nurse found venom in the puncture wound!" said the bloke in the bed.

"Nonsense, Wilberforce, I felt dense fur, it was a mole of some kind!" said another.

"Does a mole have a broad flat tail?" piped up a third. "No, it was clearly *Castor canadensis*, the North American beaver."

"Gentlemen, I don't know how to explain this . . ." began Franz, an anatomist, ". . . but the way it tracked us in the room reminded me of the electrical receptors on the elephant fish!"

They all scoffed at that.

"It was a duck," said the last one, plainly. "Don't ask how I know, it just was. I'm going home."

"The funny thing is, they were all wrong, but in some way they were all right as well!"

Q: What animal had Saltie released into the room?

The Horrifying Attack

AFTER A RATHER PERILOUS and stressful scheme, Lupin had decided to take a break from crime and spend a week in a health spa in Gérardmer in Grand Est.

He enjoyed the daily routines of mineral baths, walks by the lake and boules. One day he was passing two elderly, softly spoken gentlemen.

". . . Well, I entered the room and I found Louis Lambert splayed out with a broken spine!"

"NO! Lying on the table??"

"On the floor! Jacket covered in dirt and crumbs, and I hate to say it but there were leaves everywhere!"

The other man clutched his heart. "Horrifying! Was the culprit nearby?"

"It was Eleonora's son! He stood there with a wicked grin on his face, and . . . an appendix in his hand!"

Lupin's eyes widened involuntarily.

"The fiendish beast!" said the second man.

"And there was nothing I could do. He is only four years of age, so Eleonora wouldn't hear of any punishment!"

"Was there any chance of recovery?"

"No, only fit for worms now."

"Just not worms like us," said the other man, gravely.

Lupin thought for a moment, and then decided this was not a cause for concern.

Q: *Why wasn't Lupin concerned by their story?*

The Five Assassins

LUPIN WAS, SHALL WE say, not unaccustomed to individuals attempting to have him eliminated, whether for revenge or because his
schemes rivalled theirs. But this was the first time that five assassins had
simultaneously hired to eliminate him! They were all here in the small
fishing village of Saint-Suliac. He only knew of their presence because
he had struck up a friendship with a grizzled old local named Regale,
without knowing that he, too, was once an assassin.

"Oh yes, I have been retired for ten years but I recognized all your
friends. Cornélie, Acelin, Fitz, Bartholomew, even Emile! They are the
best in their field, monsieur, you cannot outfight them. But they each
have their weaknesses."

"Like cyanide?" Lupin asked, hiding his fear well.

"No! I mean like a hatred of bright light, or a fear of darkness. One of
them is very frightened of dogs and another is compelled to drink any
alcohol until they pass out. And the sharpest assassin is an inveterate
gambler."

"But which is which?" Lupin asked.

"Well . . ." said Regale, and then keeled forward dead, a small knife in
his back. Lupin immediately leapt over the balcony and decided a little
surveillance was in order.

Over the next week he saw Emile talking to someone about the levels
of light in his hotel, but not specifying if he wanted them to be higher
or lower. He saw Bartholomew frequent many taverns and reasoned
whatever his problem was, it was unlikely to be an issue inside a bar,
although he did show a reluctance to go inside Le Petit Chien. He
watched Cornélie's assistant deliberately take her money away, so her
problem was clearly not an issue if she had none. He heard Acelin say to
someone that as far as he was concerned blackjack was something you
hit someone with, and poker was a device for keeping a fire going. And
he noticed that Fitz always wore sunglasses.

Q: *Which assassin had which weakness?*

The Panama Guzzler

ONE OF LUPIN'S QUIRKS was that he would often assume a pseudonym that was an anagram of his own (assumed) name. Often people would be too dazzled by his current scheme to notice this, and if they did notice he would no doubt have a reason for them to do so.

One person who often noticed was Lupin's dogged pursuer Inspector Ganimard, who now whenever he met someone new would instinctively try to scramble the letters of their name in his head to see if Arsène Lupin was the result!

In one strange case, Lupin had taken the time to steal the tiara of a self-declared exiled princess. However, his true aim had been to expose her as a fraud who was using her status to extract money from impoverished French people easily taken in by her aristocratic attitude. After she had been charged and imprisoned, Lupin returned the tiara to Ganimard himself, but locked inside a small metallic box with a number code: "1 1 1 8 1 5 9 1 will open the box, you can stake my name on it!" the note declared. But that code did not work at all.

His name . . . Ganimard had noticed something strange about the pseudonym Lupin had used for this caper. He called a colleague into his office.

"Look, here are some of the false names Lupin has used. Which one strikes you as somewhat different?"

- Paul Sernine.

- Luis Perenna.

- Neil Pearsun.

- Rex Passineli.

- Sir Paul Neel.

The colleague had no idea, but as Ganimard looked at the one Lupin had used, he suddenly realized the trick. "Ah, it's not just what was taken away but what replaced it!"

He quickly entered a new number code and the box sprang open immediately!

Q: a) Which pseudonym is the odd one out?
b) What is the new number code?

Lupin's Creed

WHILE IT WAS OFTEN possible for Lupin to scale walls and climb along the outside of buildings, it was his personal belief that the inside of buildings was always preferable, especially in the case of older buildings like castles and historical monuments, which often had the tendency to crumble under unexpected weight, even if you were a trim 71 kg (156 lb) like Lupin.

Yet he found himself now up on the edge of another fragile, poorly maintained roof, looking down at a succession of weatherbeaten grotesques and gargoyles that would probably fall off as soon as he laid a hand upon them.

Except—wait—he could now see that against all odds someone had parked a small cart full of hay bales in the courtyard, almost directly below where he was. He could possibly rely on that to break his fall or, if he could get a bit lower, perhaps simply drop into it and avoid having to climb down entirely.

But from what height would it be safe for him to drop? During his time researching one of his rare, reluctant parachute drops, he learned that when a falling man reached the speed of 200 km (124 miles) travelling toward the ground, any impact would be fatal. Terminal velocity.

Lupin climbed down until he was 12 m (39 ft) above the hay bale. He calculated that he would drop for about two seconds and achieve the speed of about 55 km (34 miles) per second.

However, Lupin's weight did not include the 15 kg (33 lb) of gold bars he had strapped to his body.

Q: Can Lupin still survive the fall?

The Six Wives of Harry Butler Jr

L UPIN ONCE TOLD ME of an occasion in Paris in 1925 when he met a charming American named Harry Butler.

"Junior! Harry Butler Junior!" he insisted. "The old man was in oil. Like a sardine, hah! I make movies. Well, I make other people make movies by shouting at them. Started when I was 25, 20 years in the game . . . What's your business, Mr. Magnus?"

Lupin considered this, "I am a thief. I was thinking of robbing you."

"Is that so? Well I hate to say it but I'm flat broke. I've been married six times, you see. That's why I'm here in Paris, just finalized my sixth divorce!"

The ability of Americans to obtain quick divorces in Paris had been a recent scandal, and even by the more permissive standards of Hollywood, six wives sounded like a lot.

Harry began counting them off on his fingers. "Number one, well, she's always been my greatest weakness, we were at school together. She has these two chihuahuas . . . Number two was an actress in one of my movies, in her thirties now, very passionate, set fire to my second house. Number three, obviously I didn't learn my lesson, two chihuahuas again . . . Number four I can barely remember, she was this really young modern artist just out of her teens, and we were both pretty smashed the whole time . . . Number five was older than me but she was so smart, she ran circles round me in court. And number six, well, you know the old story, don't return to a lit firework unless you want your house full of Mexican dog hair."

Harry Butler Junior drained his gimlet cocktail thoughtfully.

"56,250 bucks, that's what they all took from me. And funnily enough the oldest woman got the most, the next youngest got half as much, and so on. Weird."

Q: *How much did the sixth wife get?*

The Fabulous Objects

"**M**ONSIEUR LUPIN . . ." said a strangely smooth voice, and Lupin turned to see Theseus, the bearded prisoner, now clean-shaven but with the same wild eyes.

"I have renounced crime, monsieur. I am now a curator of fabulous objects, and the brilliant thing is, even a master thief like yourself cannot steal them!"

Lupin was intrigued, although he remembered Theseus's previous "insights" and was appropriately wary.

"Oh yes!" shouted Theseus, disturbing a few people in the open square trying to have lunch. "The room is dark but the objects glitter enough for you to see all of them! There's a set of scales and an easel, a chemical furnace near a harp, there's an octant and a sextant, a clock with a pendulum and a clever little air pump, and don't forget the shield, or the compass for lost mariners. In fact, all the objects help those at sea!"

"And I cannot steal them?" asked Lupin.

"You can see them all but you will never be able to even touch them! There's even a telescope. The whole thing is defended by a great bear with a plough and a little bear. I will be viewing them in seven hours, and you can see them too if you want, monsieur."

Lupin knew that he would.

Q: Why can't Lupin steal these objects?

The Body of Arsène Lupin

A STIFF, PARTIALLY LIMBLESS BODY was dragged out of the Seine one misty November night. In its clothes were all the identifying marks of one individual . . . Arsène Lupin!

The youths who found the body were incredulous, part terrified, part excited by this waterlogged find. They could barely look at its glassy stare and the strangely frozen expression of malevolence.

They knew that Lupin had been active in the area recently, even going so far as to rob the Musée de la Préfecture de Police, the crime museum run by the Paris police themselves. They had just created a special exhibition of Lupin artefacts and evidence, and apparently the great thief was most displeased by what he felt was its lack of quality.

Had he come to blows with the museum's curator and been bested in combat? The body's limbs seemed to have become detached of their own accord rather than having been sliced off. And while his clothes looked to be of a fine quality, upon inspection their waterlogged state showed them to be made with a somewhat cheaper fabric.

And why would Lupin bear his own identification? Why would Lupin dress this way at all, looking exactly as they had all imagined him to appear?

In the end the police came to get the body, but their expressions were not that of triumph at the outwitting of their foe, but rather slight embarrassment, and as they carried the water-sodden body away, one of them paid the youths a franc each to never mention this to anyone.

Q: Why weren't the police happy at receiving the body?

The Haul of Le Troglodiste

ANOTHER MYSTERIOUS CRIMINAL THAT Lupin would occasionally cross paths with was Le Troglodiste, a subterranean fellow who dwelled in Paris's extensive sewer system, never seen without his distinctive froglike mask. Most of the rest of Paris's underworld avoided this denizen of the true underworld because of his scent and appearance, but also because what he valued was largely at odds with them. He enjoyed precision-made tools and machines, especially waterproof ones, but had very little interest in precious stones or gold because in the dim light of the sewer they were not shiny or beautiful at all.

It was in this spirit that at a dank crossroads in the under-tombs Lupin was able to trade two incandescent lamps of the most modern design with a cache of gems that Le Troglodiste had somehow extracted from several expensive hotel rooms using their plumbing systems.

"What do you have?" Lupin asked as Le Troglodiste excitedly toyed with one of his new lamps.

"Diamonds, sapphires, rubies, emeralds!" he muttered through his mask.

"Yes, but how many?"

"Hee hee hee! All but 11 of them are diamonds, all but 10 are sapphires, all but 12 are rubies, and all but 9 emeralds!"

Luckily Lupin was accustomed to this particularly odd way of speaking.

Q: *How many diamonds, sapphires, rubies and emeralds did Le Troglodiste have?*

The Foolish Robbers

O N ONE HOT SUMMER night, two robbers managed to lever open the window of one of Lupin's own smaller apartments and climb inside.

They peered around at the modest but tasteful decorations and tiptoed through the small kitchen where a mortar and pestle was surrounded by the remnants of fresh vegetables. One of the robbers considered trying to steal a large earthenware pot nearby, but his compatriot pointed to an adjoining room. There they noted that the small dining table was set for two and had two full bowls of soup in the places.

"Observe, Gaston," said the first. "Dinner is served. We should leave immediately lest the occupants detect us!"

"No, wait!" said Pierre, who considered himself a criminal genius. He stuck his pinky finger into one of the soup bowls and after extracting it, gave it a lick.

"Delicious! I taste tomato and cucumber, with a mix of Andalusian spices like cumin and paprika. But most importantly I note . . . it is completely cold!"

Gaston was surprised. "They have fled the apartment?"

"A long time ago. That's what I think, anyway." Pierre continued. "We may steal with impunity!"

When Lupin and his guest, a beautiful but martially skilled young Spanish lady, entered two minutes later and subdued the robbers, he was quick to inform them of their mistake.

Q: *Why does the soup being cold not indicate that they had been gone for hours?*

The Fateful Footprints

I F YOU KNEW THAT Lupin had robbed you, it was very likely he wanted you to know. Throughout the decades, many people remained ignorant that they had been robbed by the master criminal, and some did not even know they had been robbed at all, proudly displaying forgeries for the world to see (as in the Louvre . . .).

This was due to Lupin's precision of technique, and he was very strict with those who assisted him should they deviate from his proven methods. This is why when he had had to have an accomplice commit a key robbery without his assistance, the returning accomplice was so mortified.

"I committed a grievous error, master!" the accomplice panted. "I took into account your suggestion that the eastern courtyard would be less guarded. But I arrived late due to the snowfall, and the robbery took longer than I thought because my fingers were cold! As I left, the snow had stopped and I could feel it growing warmer, but it was sunrise, and a glow illuminated the ledge where you suggested I climb over the wall! Instead, I ran through the courtyard, afraid that the bright rising sun would expose me! But now I realize I left footprints all through the snow. Surely when the occupants return at lunchtime they will see them!"

Lupin smiled and slapped his friend on the back. "I do not think they will."

Q: *Why won't they see the footprints in the snow?*

The Mère de Lupin

OVER THE YEARS, MANY had claimed some connection with Lupin in the hope of gaining money or fame, or some other thing. In 1908 a woman calling herself Orianne Lupin came forward erroneously claiming to be his mother. The woman in question said she had single-handedly brought him up, only to fall into despair when he embraced a life of crime.

"It was so sad, I gave birth to my sweet Arsène exactly a year after his father died in battle in Siam! April 1874. With no family to support me, we were poor but honest. I raised him to be decent, but the streets out there are so hard."

"Quite hard," said Inspector Ganimard, who did not share the view of the more credulous public and newspapers that she was in any way plausible. "We have a record of your arrest in March 1874. Public drunkenness."

"Oh yes? It has been a hard life, I will admit. Look upon me, can you believe I am 41 years of age? Time has ravaged me."

"Perhaps the four years you spent in prison from 1896 contributed to that," said Ganimard.

"Ah yes . . . during that time my boy was looked after by my sister. Perhaps that is where he got his criminal streak!"

Ganimard escorted the woman from his room and warned her that Lupin would not look kindly on this charade and she would be better off dropping it.

Q: *Why did Ganimard not believe her story?*

The Forces of Fantômas

"HOW MANY WORK FOR your organization?" asked Lupin to the hooded monk now restrained before him. Only silence greeted his request. The monk had been caught infiltrating one of Lupin's secret hideouts, and Lupin suspected he was from the same group who operated the poisonous vineyard he had dismantled. He needed to have an idea of their numbers, so as to act appropriately.

"You are afraid of your employer, yes? Of Fantômas? He's not truly a ghost, you know, he's but a man, and a fool who is destined for failure . . ."

The monk glared at him, but Lupin, as a keen observer of people, could sense he was tired of working for Fantômas and it was only his fear that kept him silent.

"I know Fantômas has told you that if you reveal any information about your cult, you will be struck dead immediately," Lupin continued. "But perhaps there is a way you can tell me the number without saying it directly?"

The monk silently considered this, then spoke. "If you quadrupled the number of my brothers, then tripled it, then divided it into four parts, then doubled it, and then divided it by eight and added me to one of the eighths, the number would be . . . 250."

Q: *How many monks work for Fantômas?*

The Suspicions of
Monsieur Lupin

LUPIN WAS DETERMINED TO uncover the true identity of Liseron. After his rival had claimed his own identity in public, he had sought to confuse things further by putting up posters with the face of Lupin (or at least one of his recent disguises) all around Paris, accompanied by a speech balloon reading "Je suis Monsieur Liseron."

It had also eroded trust between Lupin and some of his colleagues. One young man, a skilled acrobat named Sebastian Saint Jonnison, told Lupin that during rehearsal at his circus he had seen over the wall into an adjacent garden where there was a valuable-looking silver statuette. Another contact, a crochety old antiques expert called Julius Monisse-Seronier, claimed he had been called to the house of a client and had briefly glimpsed a collection of authentic Raphael sketches. And a third individual, a corrupt policeman named Jean Moreau-Roussell, offered Lupin a chance to break into the evidence vaults of the Sûreté. They all seemed like potential traps . . .

Q: Which of these offers is in fact a trap?

The Poisoned Cup

LUPIN WAS NOT AN expert on medieval culture, though he did probably know more than your average thief. Nonetheless, he was still somewhat irked by the artificiality of the supposed medieval banquet he was attending tonight, from the garish costumes to the menu and wine choice and the attendees' conduct. This "medieval society" had been formed several years earlier by a small group of rich English landowners, but they had no interest in the actual history of the time and simply saw it as an excuse for gluttony and mischief, particularly Lord Finsdale and his right-hand man, John Brockhurst.

Lupin was there because among the dross were a few genuine pieces of value, and he wanted to liberate them. He was in the guise of one of the waiters, and somehow accidentally stumbled onto some parallel intrigue when he heard two other waiters whispering.

"The poison has been put into one of three cups."

"Who is the target—Brockhurst, Finsdale or Pertwee?"

"Finsdale. But where is the poison?"

"Listen. The pellet with the poison's in the flagon with the dragon. The vessel with the pestle and the chalice from the palace are safe."

Lupin wondered whether to intervene but decided at this point caution was best advised. The three men sat together on the central table in a row. The vessel was placed before the first, the flagon before the second, and the chalice before the third. But wait, there was some confusion! The first man said he had ordered a different wine and switched with the third. Then the second said that he had the wrong kind of wine, too, and switched with the first. Then, as they stood to see the joust, the servants secretly swapped their drinks again, so that every man had a different cup from those that they had when they had stood up. As they passed Lupin, he heard one servant whisper: "It is done, the right man *finally* has the poisoned flagon."

Q: a) In what order are Brockhurst, Finsdale and Pertwee sitting?
b) At the end, who has which cup?

The Riddle of the Castle

LUPIN MOVED THROUGH THE dark, dank catacombs of the Castillo de Sombra, kicking at the occasional rat. He could hear hundreds of them scampering around the cold stone castle, an infestation that his contact on the island said had grown incredibly over the past hundred years as they feasted on the castle's massive food supply. He just hoped they hadn't decided to chew upon the valuable documents he sought.

He made his way through its ruined halls and soiled chambers to the tower room. Countless generations of the De Sombra family had dwelled here, made merry, planned conquests and betrayed each other, but misfortune and malice had felled them, one by one, and the final living occupant of the house was a passing vagabond who had made a nest in this tower room for decades, before passing away 30 years ago.

As Lupin searched the room, he noted that the vagabond had scrawled words on the wall with charcoal:

"There are hearts that beat within these walls that bear the blood of the generations past!"

A clear sign of his madness, thought Lupin, because when the vagabond wrote that, the family were all long dead before he had even arrived. And yet . . .

Q: How is the vagabond's statement true?

The Gaulish Potion

W HILE SEARCHING FOR INFORMATION on a fabled French artefact, Lupin found a seemingly earnest document about how during the Roman Empire a small village in Gaul supposedly had a magic potion that gave people great strength and toughness. It used the properties of three berries that grew locally, which were red, blue and yellow. The problem was finding the right number of berries to add to each potion so that the Gaul was strong and tough, but didn't suffer from each berry's weird side effects.

They made a potion with one blue berry and one yellow berry. After drinking it the Gaul was strong and tough, but he grew twice as big and moved four times as slow.

Then they made a potion with one red berry and one blue berry, and after drinking it the Gaul was strong but not tough, shrank to half his size and was moving twice as fast as usual.

They tried a potion with one yellow berry and one red berry, and the Gaul who drank it was tough but not strong, moved twice as slow and was four times as small!

Q: a) What is each berry's benefit and side effects?
b) How many of each berry needs to be added to a potion to make the Gaul strong and tough, but a normal size and moving at normal speed?

Lupin's Cell

After Arsène Lupin had escaped yet another prison, the authorities insisted on having his cell thoroughly searched.

"No one has escaped this jail since the days of Louis XIV! Since the time of the Roman Empire!! Find out how he did it!" ranted the warden.

There was no evidence of his method, so the warden then insisted they look for some kind of clue as to his future plans or whereabouts. Ten minutes later one of the guards, not known for his perspicacity, entered the room breathlessly.

"I have found something but I do not understand it. Perhaps a code? Often the prisoners will count off their days here with straight lines—they draw four lines, then cross through them with a fifth . . ."

"I understand what tally marks are, you fool, go on!"

"Well, Lupin has done something like that, with lines, but the marks are strange. Some of them come to a point at the bottom, others cross each other left to right. Some almost look like letters! They cannot be numbers, they must be . . ."

The warden held up his hand. "They are numbers."

Q: In what way are the lines numbers?

The Miraculous Walk

LUPIN TOLD ME VARIOUS contradictory stories of his beginning in crime, although later I realized they were in fact just different facets of a singular origin.

One time he told me of his youth in Paris, committing mere petty crimes like stealing food or tormenting members of the Sûreté.

"In the winter of 1891 the cops had had enough of my antics. They arranged a trap: a temptingly lost young aristocrat walking along the Quai d'Austerlitz idly staring at the Seine River, with a bulging pocketbook practically hanging out of his jacket. I was so foolish then, I trailed him and pounced, but he was of course an undercover officer and there were eight of his compatriots in the shadows. I froze, but then I bolted! Naturally, they had men posted on the bridge and I saw no possible escape, but then I became aware that something had changed, and I walked across the Seine!"

I spluttered at this. "You . . . walked on water?"

Lupin waved his hand dismissively, "I am not claiming magical powers. But I walked across the Seine. A foolish big-bellied officer who tried to follow me ended up in the water, and by the time his colleagues had retrieved his freezing shivering form, I was on the other side. That's when I realized the prospects of crime!"

Q: How did Lupin walk across the Seine?

The House of the Nemesis

LUPIN'S MATHEMATICIAN FRIEND DAVID Hilbert was often amazed by some of Lupin's tales, particularly those where he faced his foes.

"Have you any adversaries, David?" Lupin asked playfully.

"In a way, yes," Hilbert said. "In fact, in a strange coincidence my worst enemy lives in a house whose number is my own house number reversed. Can you tell what the numbers are?"

Lupin considered this. "Can you give me any clues?"

"Well, both our house numbers are prime numbers. And if you add the two digits together you get a higher number than if they were multiplied by each other."

"Who is this enemy of yours?"

Hilbert smiled. "He is a man, my age, and he has stood in my way for as long as I can remember. His foolish decisions always cause me pain . . ."

Q: What is the number of Hilbert's worst enemy's house?

Rochambord's Birthday Gift

A S PART OF PREPARATION for a robbery Lupin had befriended an aristocrat, but had found himself strangely sympathetic toward the man, as it seemed no one liked him or had regard for him despite his conduct being fairly reasonable compared to many of the men of his station.

"It's my family's history, very tangled and scandalous, even for France," Rochambord mused sadly. "My best friend was the Comte de Brasselon, and when his father died in a shooting accident, I found myself . . . drawn to his mother. She's a beautiful woman, a wonderful soul. We married that spring and he gave his consent, but seemed resentful. Then, strangely, my own father died the next year in a similar hunting accident! And before you knew it, the Comte was courting my own mother!"

"As . . . revenge?" Lupin asked, not really wanting to know the answer.

"He swore that it was a genuine love match! Perhaps he is right. They are still married now. But I suspected he had killed my father, and it came out that he suspected me of killing his, so we don't communicate now, even though we are technically each other's . . . step-fathers."

Rochambord took a sip of wine. "The only person who gives me a birthday gift is my step-grandfather." And he laughed bitterly.

Q: *Who is Rochambord's step-grandfather?*

The Socialist Highwayman

ONE OF LUPIN'S OTHER colleagues was a politically active young man named Rogier Moreau. He was very insistent that any money gathered from robberies was shared equally amongst everyone in the group.

"My beliefs may seem modern, but in fact they have been in my family for generations! My great-grandfather Denis was a highwayman in France, which as you know was a very perilous undertaking with the Maréchaussée riding around policing the roads! He was so poor he could not even afford a gun; he simply kept his hand in his pocket, but he was so fierce everyone believed he was armed!"

"And he robbed the rich to give to the poor?" said Lupin sardonically.

"Oh no, he was even fairer than that! If he robbed a carriage, he would force everyone there to share out their valuable items equally so that they all had the same amount! For example, once he stopped a carriage with four occupants: a rich Count, his spoiled daughter, a more disadvantaged doctor and, of course, the carriage driver. The count had 60 francs, the daughter a charm bracelet with six charms each worth 5 francs, so 30 francs. The doctor had a medical bag with a stethoscope, lancet, bandages, morphine and surgical spirit, 25 francs all told. And the carriage driver had his most valuable item, a pocket watch worth 10 francs. And he made them share everything out equally, even though one of them did not share anything!"

Q: How can the people share so that everyone has items of equal worth?

The Pale Workman

WHEN YOUNGER, LUPIN TOILED for three months as a workman on the construction of the wing of an art museum. During this time he developed a healthy tan from the outdoor work, and when he frequented worker's bars with his new friends in the evening, he noted that everyone there was the same, except for one man who was almost deathly pale.

"Is he a worker?" Lupin asked with curiosity.

"Oh yes, he works very hard!" said one of his friends. "He probably works harder than any of us, so much digging and hauling."

"But he is inside all of the time?" said Lupin as he stared at the yawning man who was eating a croissant.

"No, outside, very much outside, in all weathers!" said his friend.

"And is he covered up the whole time?"

"No, he prefers to be uncovered unless it gets colder. If he wore a cloak it might upset some people to see him! Not that there are many around where he works."

"And he works alone?" said Lupin, noting that he was the only pale man here.

"Not exactly. I would say that he has many people around him, but they are not talkative at all!"

"And they don't come here?"

"No, they are very committed to staying at his worksite! Their positions there are set in stone, as it were . . ."

Q: *Why does the pale worker not have a tan like the others?*

The Mobius Safe

I N ONE OF HIS most hidden lairs, Lupin kept a safe that he could not crack. He had found it in the catacombs of a strange mathematical cult that worshipped someone called Murray Arte. Oh, he could have broken open its shell with tools, or tried to blow a hole in it with dynamite, but he chose not to as its construction was so devious that he coveted the safe itself far more than whatever was inside.

The safe had a dial that had the numbers 1–20 on it. Whichever number was selected meant that the dial had to be turned forward by that amount, so on 1 you would move forward one space to 2, on 2 you would move it forward two spaces to 4. On 4 you would go to 8 etc. But when you landed on 16, you had to move the dial sixteen spaces forward past the 20, and all the way back around to 12. If you landed on 18, you would move the dial eighteen places forward and land on 16.

> Q: Is there a number that you can start from which
> will bring the dial back to 1?

The Museum Mystery

YOU ARE ONCE AGAIN called to the scene of a crime. It is the Musée des Arts et Métiers in Paris, a museum dedicated to the history of science. You walk past cases displaying scientific instruments and samples from over a hundred years of progress.

"The people gathered here were part of an exclusive soirée to celebrate the restoration of the famed 'Foucault's Pendulum' exhibit, until they suddenly became aware that their personal items were disappearing! What Lupin did not anticipate was that we received a tip-off about his plans and we have had the entire party under surveillance. The building is surrounded, and after vetting the other guests we can say with certainty that someone in that room is Arsène Lupin!"

As you enter the room your eyes are immediately drawn to the large pendulum in the middle of the room, still swinging around, surrounded by a mock-up of Foucault's lab complete with a mannequin of the man himself, and glass cases with some of his more valuable instruments. Milling around were four individuals:

- The German industrialist Hans Kreisler, wiping his shiny bald head with a handkerchief.
- Mademoiselle Langoustine, the circus performer and chanteuse, a remarkably tall lady.
- Charles Dubonner, a failed poet who had been working as a waiter at the event and had a strangely dark moustache for a man of his hair colour.
- Professor Michael Dunwitty, an Irish scientific historian whose speciality was Foucault.

"Ridiculous, this all is," said Kreisler. "I do not mean your interrogation, I mean this display! I told them I did not want such mummery as a waxwork or a model of his laboratory! Just the pendulum!"

"Actually I consulted on the laboratory design," said Dunwitty, seemingly offended, "although I had no responsibility for the waxwork. The clothes are correct but it looks nothing like him."

"Will this take long?" asked Mademoiselle Langoustine as a policeman

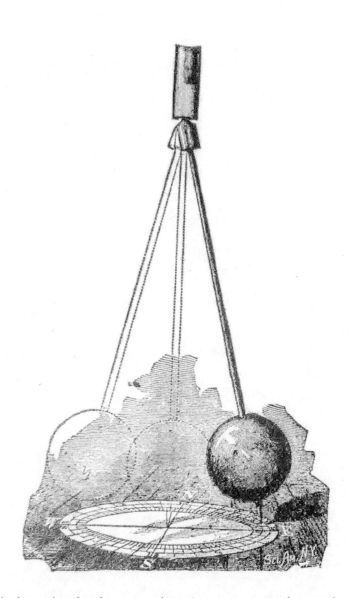

checked Kreisler's head to ensure he was not wearing makeup. "I have to attend another pendulum unveiling on the other side of the city."

Dubonner had been quite silent but when you asked about his moustache he sheepishly peeled it off, then removed his eyebrows and hair as well. "I have been entirely hairless from birth, monsieur. My mother was startled by a walrus when I was in her belly."

Q: Who in the room is Lupin?

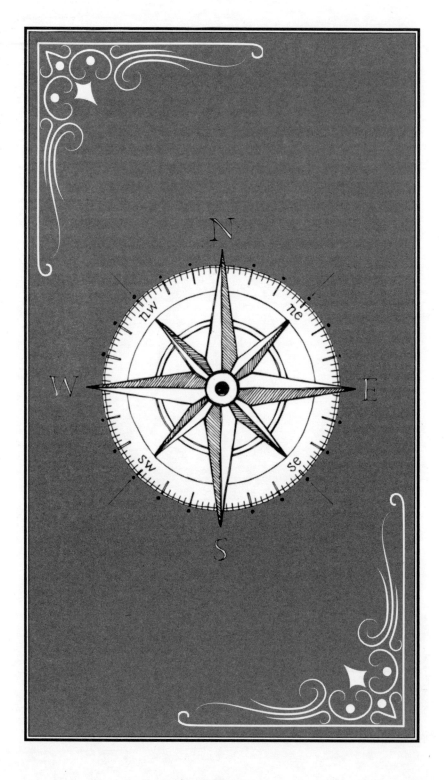

The Compass in the Courtyard

I CAN'T SAY THAT LIFE with Monsieur Lupin wasn't exciting! This one time we were robbing this fort deep in the Pyrenees. We finish grabbing what we want and then Lupin rappels down off a balcony into the courtyard to get our escape vehicle. Well, he didn't reckon on the specially drugged meat he had given the dogs wearing off so quickly—they came haring after him with their slavering jaws snapping after his legs.

"Reginald!" he shouts, and then he mimes to me that he's pulling a lever. I look next to me and I see in the wall there are four levers with a "o" at the bottom and a "ı" at the top. But I don't know the code so I just shrug!

He points frantically at the floor of the courtyard where there's a mosaic of the compass, you know: Nord, Est, Sud and Oest, as the French have it, with the N at the top. Then he starts dashing round the courtyard very precisely, he goes left, then toward the upper right corner, then left again, then up, then right, then goes to the upper left corner, then up, right, left, and upper right corner. I thought about it, and then turned the first two levers and the last lever up, leaving the third one down. The trapdoor opened and Lupin jumped through!

Later I said he could have just held up some fingers, and he gave me a very sour look.

Q: How did Reginald know which levers to pull?

The Fencing Matches

ONE AREA IN WHICH Lupin felt he needed improvement was the art of sword-fighting. As ridiculous as it seemed for this to be a part of his repertoire in the age of the pistol, he found himself in sword fights so frequently that he thought he should polish up a bit. For this reason he attended an international fencing tournament to see if he could find a suitable tutor, but the fighters were all so equally matched he could not decide and began to become bored. Then he discovered something strange: as he looked at the list of nine bouts, he realized it formed a pattern, although if the pattern continued, the tenth bout could not take place . . .

- DeSmet vs Frelupt.
- Von Blyenburgh vs DeSmet.
- Stuyck vs DeSchepper.
- DeSmet vs Stuyck.
- Von Blyenburgh vs Frelupt.
- Stuyck vs DeSmet.
- DeSmet vs DeSchepper.
- Von Blyenburgh vs Stuyck.
- Stuyck vs Frelupt.

Q: a) What is the pattern?
b) Why could the tenth bout not take place?

The Enormous Darkness

AFTER HE HAD ROBBED the Eiffel Tower, Lupin made a point of giving some of the money to Pierre Falmont, a man he knew who despised the tower, not for its aesthetics or any cultural objection, but for one specific reason.

"The shadow of that behemoth has stolen the sunlight my garden used to enjoy!" Pierre had grumbled to Lupin as they sat in a small brasserie. "I do not care for its appearance, true, but the darkness it casts is the true curse that it puts upon Paris."

"Your part of Paris, perhaps!" grunted Luigi Vercotti, Pierre's best friend and nemesis, as he swivelled around on his stool. "The shadow it casts is nothing compared to that of the Mole Antonelliana! An immense lump of architecture, its shadow is like a massive cloak of blackness thrown upon whatever stands at its feet."

"I have been witness to a worse shadow," said Lupin, in the spirit of competition. "The shadow that this thing casts is so immense that it projects darkness across hundreds of thousands of kilometres! A shadow so great that it even causes darkness to fall upon itself."

The two old men fell silent in contemplation of this.

"Strangely, though . . ." he continued, ". . . this shadow is only visible to us at night!"

Q: *What thing is Lupin speaking about?*

The Go-between

L UPIN OFTEN HELD THAT his compatriot Rogier Moreau was overly
dedicated to equality. "I like to help those who need it, after I've
helped myself, of course, but all this redistribution just causes problems,
like those in Russia."

Moreau shook his head. "Not at all, in fact I have brought peace
between two of France's most notorious street gangs. On Corsica, the
Warriors and the Sharks each dominated their respective towns, but
they had been bristling against each other's territory for months and
declared an enormous fight at a place equidistant between the towns,
to settle it once and for all. They started marching to the place from
opposite directions and I only found out about this when they were
8 km apart! I knew it would be a bloodbath. I had to negotiate peace,
but I knew as soon as they got together their anger would prevail.

Both groups were moving slowly, about 4 kph, so I grabbed my new
bicycle, as I knew I could cycle at about 24 kph! I cycled back and forth
between the two groups, shouting messages. Every time I got to them I
would have to turn back around and immediately cycle back. But by the
time they met at the square all problems were resolved and they shook
hands! And I collapsed."

Lupin found the story unlikely, but was amused. "How far do you
think you cycled that day?"

Q: How far do you think Moreau cycled that day?

The Mystery of the Legionnaires

F OR SOME TIME AFTER an adventure that led to a tragic outcome he regretted, Lupin joined the French Foreign Legion, under a pseudonym he neglected to tell me. He said it was in a way refreshing for him, as a man of so many false names (including Arsène Lupin) to be surrounded by others in the same situation.

The Foreign Legion allowed those who were not French citizens to fight for France, and also in many situations reinvent their life and leave their past behind. For his part, Lupin tried not to pry into the pasts of his fellow legionnaires. But it was impossible for him to deactivate every part of his mind, and one day when a group of four new Legionnaires arrived he took note.

One of them, "Jacques," had yellow-stained fingers, and Lupin could detect particles in his hair that he first thought was sand, but later noted had a lighter texture. He also kept putting any writing implements behind his ear.

The second, "Pierre," had dark-rimmed eyes that the other men mocked him for, as well as black under his fingernails, and he seemed to be constantly squinting, especially when the sky was clear.

The third, "Alphonse," was very skilled at running and would often volunteer to move messages around, smoothly and swiftly conveying them from place to place. He was often so impatient between errands that he would stand tapping his foot.

The fourth, "Françoise," was also unable to remain still, often swaying from his left foot to his right as he stood. He was, however, popular with the others as he would complete manual tasks with his strong right arm on their behalf.

The fifth, "René," seemed the oldest, with a red and wrinkly face, but claimed he was younger than the others. His arms were equally strong but he often refused to bare them, saying they "told too much of his story," and while he would remain still while standing, he walked with a side-to-side gait.

Based on his observations, Lupin felt sure that these men were once a tennis player, a coal miner, a carpenter, a sailor and a dancer.

Q: Based on their quirks, which man had which occupation?

The Bizarre Robbery

T HEY COULD HARDLY BELIEVE it . . . the Paris police had managed, against all odds, to plant a radio transmitter in one of Lupin's lairs and was now able to listen in to Lupin and two compatriots as they planned their latest robbery! What seemed like the whole of the force gathered around the small set to listen in.

"Grognard, Reginald, we must decide what we need for our new venture," said a voice that they recognized as Lupin's. "I shall begin: we need guns!"

"Very good," said Grognard, ". . . and I say that we need rope."

"That makes sense," said Reginald. "And we'll need some lamps as well."

"Of course!" said Lupin. "And we will require a rickshaw!"

"Yes, and an egg whisk," said Grognard.

"Not to mention an umbrella," said Reginald.

The policemen listening in were very confused about what this robbery entailed.

"We will definitely need some oranges," said Lupin.

"Oh, and a giraffe!" said Grognard.

"Don't forget the penguin!" said Reginald.

It was at this point that the police officers realized that Lupin's gang knew that the transmitter was there . . .

Q: *What are the rules of the game that Lupin, Grognard and Reginald are playing?*

The Birthday Gold

L UPIN WOULD BE THE first to admit when he had been fooled or had misjudged a venture, and the Saute fortune was one of them.

"It was widely known that Marguerite Saute had a huge fortune in gold kept in a Swiss bank account," said Lupin. "She was by all measures a kind person, but her children were not, and so I resolved that as soon as she passed, I would clear out the account before her undeserving progeny could swoop in. And so in 1912, when she died at the age of 76, I set my plans."

He sighed. "The whole operation was extremely complex and required a large outlay of money on my part, and the result . . . well. Let me just say that it turned out that from the age of 20, every birthday she had, Marguerite Saute had put 1,000 francs in gold bullion into this account. However, it also appeared that she loved her older sister Gina, and on every birthday Gina had, Marguerite would withdraw 300 francs to buy her an elaborate gift—her only withdrawal, but a withdrawal nonetheless."

"I see . . . but surely that still leaves a considerable amount."

Lupin shook his head. "In fact there were only 2,200 francs left. And no one else had even touched the account."

Q: *Why was such a small amount left in the account?*

The Unwanted Visitor

L UPIN WAS AWARE THAT the public view of his life no doubt suggested
a non-stop whirlwind of visits to the most exclusive hotels and
glamorous luxury castles. While that was definitely true some of the
time, on this occasion he was sitting in the drawing room of a rundown
low-class Pension, a boarding house at Number 3 rue du Chevalier-de-
La-Barre, warming himself by the fire as the rain pelted down outside.

He pretended not to listen as a woman with wet hair and clothes
remonstrated with the owner. Apparently a guest of this house had just
knocked on her door. When she answered, he had claimed that he was
mistaken and he'd thought it was his room, as it had the number two on
it. She said that it was impossible he would make this mistake. She said
that she had tolerated other problems before, like the noise late at night,
but this was the last straw!

Lupin had seen the man she had mentioned earlier with the companion
with whom he was sharing the room, and he had noted that the number
on their key was indeed two. But he, too, was certain that, for obvious
reasons, it had not been a mistake.

Q: *Why was Lupin certain this was not a mistake?*

The Failing Montgolfière

T HE ONLY TIME THAT Lupin attempted an escape via hot air balloon definitely indicated to him that it was not going to be one of his preferred methods moving forward.

It had started well, as he had disguised it as a promotional stunt for a new pleasure park that was opening on the border of France and Belgium. He had grabbed the treasures and jumped in, confident that the locals would have no way of pursuing him once he had entered the cloud cover and gone past the mountains. However his montgolfière was defective and began losing altitude, bringing him closer to the ground and the crowd of angry people directly underneath the balloon.

Seven yards from the ground, Lupin decided he had to act. There were eight things in the balloon, and for it to begin rising again he would have to jettison exactly 65 kg of weight, and he only had time to throw out two things.

In the balloon he had:

- An anchor, 20 kg.
- A gold salver, 5 kg.
- A rope, 3 kg.
- A gilded bronze bust of Napoleon, 30 kg.
- An Emmanuel gilt ottoman, 10 kg.
- An 18th-century Spanish studded leather chest filled with silver ducats, 32 kg.
- A Tang Dynasty iron horse statue, 4 kg.

Q: *Which two things need to leave the balloon to allow Lupin the best chance of escape?*

The Pearl of Ischia

LUPIN MAY BE KNOWN for some of the most audacious and elaborate plots, but he also kept his ears open for opportunities wherever he found himself. During one of the very brief times he was in the United States, he took the chance to visit California to see the new mechanical racing track they had installed. As he passed through the crowd, he suddenly heard people talking.

"The Pearl of Ischia! Completely gone!" said a panicked woman. "All I found was a broken chain!"

"We have to start searching," said a similarly frantic man. "Give out a description. Um . . . white, with a natural glossy sheen . . ."

"We could say cultivated, rather than wild . . ."

"No, that doesn't matter! Just think of appearance."

The woman looked thoughtful. "What about the mother-of-pearl?"

"We could look there, I suppose. Oh, it's worthless, the pearl is one of a kind, some robber has definitely . . ."

"You can bet on it," he said. "He'll move fast and make real money for someone."

The lady sniffed. "Yes, the pearl always looked good on an oval . . ."

Suddenly the woman saw something in the crowd and pointed, and the two ran off. When Lupin saw what they were moving toward, he smiled. Not a gemstone after all . . .

Q: What is the Pearl of Ischia?

The Venetian Escape

L UPIN'S REPUTATION RELIED IN some way on him being able to achieve the impossible and be both very unpredictable and also supposedly very predictable. These were not always compatible aims, but they certainly made for amusing and entertaining claims from him, regarding the nature of his adventures.

For example, I was having lunch with him when he overheard two young men on the adjoining table planning their trip to Venice.

"Oh, and Gussy, remember, there are no roads in Venice, so you can't go haring around in your automobile like you normally do!" one of them said.

"I suppose that would reduce your ability to escape in a crisis," I commented to Lupin idly.

"Oh, in fact I did escape from a gang of marauders using a car while in Venice," Lupin said with a similar level of casualness.

"What was this, a car that could run on water?" I joked.

"Not at all. A real car with wheels and an engine."

"Then I suppose you were on the outskirts of the city and escaped by driving away."

"No, this was in the middle of the city. I had just used the opportunity of a film première, the first showing of the popular *Keystone Cops* shorts in Italy. They had brought a lot of visually exciting elements to help draw in the crowds and it was the perfect opportunity for me to snatch a particular necklace I sought, but somehow they became aware of my actions and a chase ensured, not unlike those in the film! Suddenly I realized that they lost track of where I was, so I took the chance to leap into the car and through that means I was able to escape."

"Did they chase you? Was it difficult to drive?"

"Not at all. I didn't even have to take any turns."

"You can't have been able to go very fast?"

"That's true. And yet after a couple of hours I had totally eluded them."

Q: *How was Lupin able to use a car to escape in Venice?*

The Fountain of Youth

L UPIN'S NEMESIS AND GREATEST love, Joséphine Balsamo, was also known as Countess Cagliostro and frequently claimed to have been born in 1788 as Joséphine Pellegrini, the daughter of Count Alessandro di Cagliostro, the self-declared magician and adventurer. She said she had achieved eternal youth by some magical or mystical means, much in the same way her supposed "father" had in the 18th century. Lupin considered this to all be part of her web of deception, although he thought it possible she could be descended from the original Joséphine.

"Yes indeed, we have seen some strange things in our time," said Grognard, his companion. "But the notion of some fountain of youth or philosopher's stone that grants immortal youth is too fanciful."

"Indeed? " said Lupin with a smile. "I know for a fact that there was a man named Nikolaos who was 45 years old in 1900, but in 1910 he was 35 years old."

"Pfft!" said Grognard. "Lies!"

"It is in fact a hundred percent true."

Q: If what Lupin says is true, how can Nikolaos be 45 in 1910
but 35 in 1920?

The Fortunate Gallery

Every time a new gallery of considerable size opened in France, Lupin would visit. He was a connoisseur of both art and crime, and for him these were the greatest intersections of them. Some galleries would show classical works and antiquities, others would proudly show the newest, sometimes shocking art. Some galleries would be filled with paintings and sculptures from a diverse number of different artists, and others would concentrate on a singular figure. The gallery he visited today was primarily the work of a single and prolific artist whose work, while well regarded, was valued at only middling prices. Lupin took a stroll through the rooms, taking care to personally observe both the security measures and the nature of the brightly dressed patrons, before concluding it was not worth his time to rob the place, and he left thinking that the gallery would probably be forced to close within a few months.

One week later Lupin revisited the gallery and, although nothing of what was inside had changed, the value of its contents and the desirability of his robbing it had increased massively. As he moved among the darkly clad visitors, he noted the gallery had also increased its levels of security, but not to such an extent that Lupin could not come in the night and help himself, to possibly corner the market in the limited supply of these paintings.

Q: *Why has the value of the paintings risen so much in one week?*

Orchestral Manoeuvres in the Dark

L UPIN PREFERRED TO STEAL from the privileged and not from those in greater need. Musicians would usually fall into the latter group. The members of the Orchestre Lamoureux were fairly well paid by the standards of the time, but in normality none of them would have anything that Lupin would want. Until, that is, he became aware that one of the orchestra members owned a Stradivarius violin, built by Antonio Stradivari in 1726, absolutely priceless and exquisitely made. In the form of one of his alternate identities, Lupin made overtures toward buying it from this surprisingly muscular musician, but they were not interested. In fact, they seemed rather hostile, and not seeking to get beaten on by the musician's big powerful forearms, Lupin withdrew and decided upon stealth.

The musician had the violin locked up with sophisticated security but it was nothing compared to the skills of Lupin, and he took it with ease. The remarkable thing, however, is that despite this, the orchestra still played with a full complement 15 minutes later, even though the musician in question did not get a replacement violin from anywhere.

Q: How did all the musicians in the orchestra play without the violin being replaced?

The Locked Room Misery

S OMETIMES PEOPLE INVITED LUPIN to try and rob them, whether through arrogance, need for attention, or a strange admiration for him and his work. Often Lupin would simply ignore such entreaties as beneath him or as obvious bait. But he did not do so with Valmont Beauséjour.

Beauséjour owned a company named Goliath Sécurité, which promised that no thief could ever steal from you if they provided their services—even the amazing Arsène Lupin. To this end, Beauséjour filled a particular room in his house with very valuable items: an antique George III mahogany breakfront cabinet from 1812 in the corner, a Yuan dynasty vase from the 14th century on the mantelpiece, and a 17th-century Italian hand-carved walnut armchair by the bookshelves.

He then designed the room to have all of his latest security devices, from hermetically sealed doors to windows with thick, indestructible bars and electrified defence! All the ledges and possible access ways to the room were lined with barbed wire and spikes, and the only door was guarded at all times by Beauséjour's elite guards, unbribable and impeccably trained.

Beauséjour boasted that Lupin could never even enter the room, let alone steal anything. "I have valued the contents of this room at 500,000 francs, Monsieur Lupin!" he said at a press conference.

"You may even come to my courtyard and see its treasures through the window, but I guarantee that one week from now, when I remove the contents, the room's value will be exactly the same! You do not have a shot at entering it!"

Lupin examined the room and all its measures, its position in the house, the integrity of his guards, and concluded . . . that Beauséjour was right! He even considered trying to catapult himself into the room. But he could not enter.

Despite this, one week later, when Beauséjour opened the room, he found his guarantee had been worthless. The room's value had dropped by at least 100,000 francs and his security company's fortunes were shattered, Goliath brought down by the unlikely David that was Arsène Lupin.

Q: How did Lupin bring the contents of the room's value down without ever entering it?

The Mobile Horde

AFTER A WHILE, THOSE who had valuables and wanted to protect them from Lupin tried to find ever more devious ways of moving their property. One surprising idea that a businessman had while moving was to conceal his valuables inside a false . . . dead elephant! Lupin had to concede it was a new idea, especially as the businessman in question was a famed lover of animals. The man commissioned the construction and painting of an immense elephant corpse and then fabricated a story that it had been rescued from a foreign zoo but was sadly still too ill to survive. No such elephant had existed, but it was a good ruse nonetheless. The only issue was what he could pack inside. He needed to fill it with special toughened crates, each of which could fit eight large boxes of his items or ten smaller boxes of items. Ultimately, he managed to get 96 boxes inside his pretend pachyderm, more large than small.

Q: If he sent 96 boxes and there were more large than small, how many crates did he use?

The Unreliable Donor

G ROGNARD, LUPIN'S MOST RELIABLE associate, had much of his boss's insight into human conduct, and a keen eye for a con man. This is why Lupin was surprised when Grognard loaned 100 francs to his friend Bernard, with the understanding that Bernard would pay him back in a week.

"Bernard is one of the most disreputable people we know, Grognard, and we are both master criminals! The most substantial difference between us is that he has not a penny to his name and does not earn any money, merely spends it on wine and gambling—and women who enjoy wine and gambling!"

"I know this, Lupin, but he is my friend. That has meaning."

"Here's a wager, then, Grognard. In a week's time if Bernard hands you 100 francs, not a penny more or less, I will give you 1,000 francs."

"OK, I will take that bet!"

Over that week Lupin had Bernard monitored and, as he thought, the man passed the time buying extravagant food and alcohol, betting on boxing matches and races, and frittering away the 100 francs Grognard had given him. During this time, Bernard earned no other money.

And yet, when the day came, Lupin witnessed Bernard handing Grognard 100 francs, and was forced to pay him 1,000.

"That was a very sneaky way to win the bet," said Lupin as he paid his friend.

"Well, you did not say I couldn't talk to him beforehand," pointed out Grognard. "And you should have been more careful in how you worded the bet . . ."

Q: *How did Grognard win the bet?*

The Tempestuous Scene

LUPIN'S LIFE WAS NOT so filled with drama that he couldn't appreciate seeing it when it played out before him, and this was the case when he was a witness to a man and woman having an enormous argument while sitting at a café table.

"I saw you with Alphonse—do not pretend that you have not been with him!" the young man shouted.

"Is it wrong to seek the arms of a kind young man when another is so cruel and unfaithful!" she replied passionately.

It continued in this way, revelations and secrets flying back and forth with gusto. Lupin was riveted, and he was not the only person watching this scene. He could not say what would happen next, it was so unpredictable!

However, despite this, at one moment during the argument the woman suddenly stopped. Then a man who no one had yet seen walked up to her and solemnly handed her a piece of paper. Written on this paper, somehow, was the exact next thing she said!

Q: *How did the man know what she was going to say next?*

The Forged Certificate

AFTER ALMOST BEING TAKEN in by a series of very clever forgeries, Lupin resolved to try to track down Le Style—not to eliminate him but to try to reason with him, as he felt that they could reach a compromise and Le Style's talents were too great to waste on bitterness.

One day he thought he had found Le Style and arranged to come face to face with him in his apartment, but when he arrived he realized he had been duped. The individual was indeed a self-declared forger, but he was a particularly bad one. Le Style had guided him to a poor forgery of himself!

"I am *not* a bad forger!" said the man, named Théophile, when Lupin met him. "Yes, perhaps my eyesight is not great and my materials are unorthodox. I did not realize Ming vases were made of porcelain and not clay, I will admit that. But I have had some success! For example, this Crédit Foncier Argentin certificate that you say is sloppily printed and looks like it is on toilet paper? I took one just like it to the bank just up the road, and when I handed it over they accepted it willingly. They were very happy about the situation. I had had problems before with them but at this bank they seemed pleased to have my custom and even wanted me to establish a new account with all my personal details!"

Lupin nodded knowingly, and then left fairly soon after.

Q: Why did the bank willingly and happily accept Théophile's badly forged share certificate?

The Unacceptable Money

TWO WEEKS LATER, LUPIN finally tracked down the real Le Style, after a series of convincing replicas of 18th-century Willow pattern plates were found to feature the image of a popular seafood restaurant in Nice. Lupin met Le Style there, finding him much less bombastic and quite diminished.

"I am no longer working with Liseron, if you were curious. I wanted to strike a blow to France, but Liseron's methods and plans . . . unsettled me. Though I will not tell you what they are, if you ask. Nor will I reveal Liseron's identity. I will not break that oath."

"I fully understand," said Lupin, "but will you work with me?"

"I am retiring," said Le Style. "I perfected the art of reproduction but never created anything new. I am starting a small farm near Shchaslyvtseve."

"Surely there is some field of forgery that you have not tried?" Lupin suggested.

"No, I have mastered them all. I found bank notes strangely elusive, but once I got the correct green ink and cotton mix, they look perfect. Although, despite being indistinguishable from the original, they would not be accepted in any shops here in France . . ."

Q: *Why would Le Style's banknotes not be accepted in France?*

The Greenhouse

L UPIN WOULD SOMETIMES NEED to consult with experts about plants and flowers, whether to create an effective but ultimately harmless sleeping draught or to understand whether a particular vine on a castle would bear his weight. To this end he had struck up a friendship (under a pseudonym) with a shy but sharply intelligent young botanist called Madame Geneviève de Barre. He met her in her greenhouse.

"Oh my goodness, Monsieur Sernine! I was not expecting you today. I am tending to my favourite plants. I know I should not have favourites, but it is difficult."

Shly averting her eyes from him, she wandered over to the end of the greenhouse where seven plants lay in a row.

"They are all so interesting. This is emerald vine, *Strongylodon macrobotrys*. It is usually pollinated by bats in the Philippines. Then there is golden pothos, *Epipremnum aureum*. Cats and dogs will die if they eat it, poor dears. Oh, here is blue morning glory, *Ipomoea indica*. Aren't its heart-shaped leaves lovely? And Lady Banks' rose, *Rosa banksiae*, named after the wife of Sir Joseph Banks, my personal hero. See the little yellow flowers? Oh, and this plant, monkey cups, *Nepenthes*. They sound so jolly but they're actually carnivorous—you see, little insects drown in these pitchers of fluid. Then the sweet pea, *Lathyrus odoratus*. I'm sure you've seen these with their pink flowers. And then there's the bee orchid, *Ophrys apifera*, so extraordinary. It, uh, makes itself look like a bee to attract them, lure them in."

And she blushed.

Q: *Using the following clues, can you work out the order of the plants from 1-7?*

• *The even-numbered plants all have vowels at the beginning of their Latin names.*

• *The three plants with colours in their names are next to each other.*

• *The two plants with animals in their names are at the end.*

• *The plant with leaves shaped like a certain suit of cards is second in the line.*

• *The fifth plant is named after a person.*

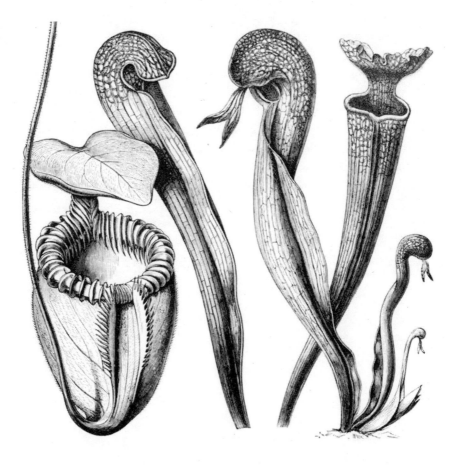

The Perfect Victim

L UPIN CONSIDERED BLACKMAIL TO be a useful tool in the construction of a larger scheme, but distasteful to be used as a primary or singular source of income. Most blackmailers were grubby, mean people, so sometimes Lupin deliberately targeted them for thefts.

One of them, a man called Sir Noel H. Derringer, surprised Lupin by having considerably less money than he thought he would, to such an extent that Lupin almost felt sympathy for him and sat down to hear his story.

"I had found the perfect victim. He was the son of a prominent member of the clergy, an archbishop, a man very dedicated to morals and ethics but with big coffers. His son portrayed himself as similarly worthy but was secretly dedicated to every vice you could imagine. Once I began blackmailing him, he would pay up regularly—he had a large stipend. Then I realized that he was gambling so much that he might lose all of his money on it, so I swiftly forced all the local bookmakers to refuse his bets. I noted he would get drunk and get into fights, and feared he would be stabbed or drown in the gutter, so I took to secretly poisoning his alcohol so that it made him feel sick, and encouraging him to attend church instead. His opium habit increased so I arranged for him to go cold turkey, and I also reasoned he should improve his diet with less fatty foods. Then, suddenly, he told me he would no longer pay me!"

Q: *Why did the young man stop paying Sir Derringer's blackmail money?*

The Golden Trap

LUPIN AWOKE. SOMEHOW, SOMEONE had got the drop on him when he had been robbing a cache of gold belonging to an idle aristocrat. It had not seemed like an obvious trap, everything had checked out, and yet the instant he went inside he felt a sharp jab on his neck and all went black.

When he awoke, he was in a sealed room.

"Good evening, Monsieur Lupin," said a strange distorted voice. "I am Liseron. I know how much you love gold, so let us test your famous acuity, no? Before you are seven gold bars. Actually, six of them are pure gold, and one is 99 percent gold and 1 percent lead. Once you find the imperfect bar, post it through the slot in the wall and you will be freed!"

Lupin detected a rank yet sweet scent in the air.

"Ah yes, can you smell the perfume? A special concoction of my own, paralysis in 1 minute and death in 2! But I am not cruel, I have given you a set of scales too . . ."

Lupin spotted the scales, bolted to the floor and wired up with dynamite.

"But if you attempt to use them more than twice, they will cease to exist. As will you, I suspect. Follow your greed, Monsieur Lupin, *bon chance!*"

Q: *How can Lupin discern which is the slightly lighter bar if he can only use the scales twice?*

The Helms of the Red Death

LUPIN AND TWO ALLIES, Grognard and Perceval, had finally infil-trated the lair of Fantômas and his sinister cult, dressing up in the monks' distinctive outfits and joining them deep in the bowels of the city. They moved with the rest of the monks to an underground auditorium where one by one they took their place at seats around a central stage marked with occult symbols. Perceval sat behind Lupin, and Grognard sat behind him, so as not to be associated with each other.

Suddenly the room went totally dark. A sinister voice said, "Brothers, don your helms."

Lupin could sense that around him each monk was reaching beneath his seat and pulling out some kind of helm, like a knight's helmet. Lupin felt beneath his seat and found a full helm and, with some trepidation, pulled it over his head. Then suddenly there was a great rush of people.

Before Lupin could move, the lights snapped back on. The seats all around him were empty. He could not see Grognard or Perceval, but could tell they were still seated behind him. Standing on the stage was Fantômas in a distinctive, twisted purple demon mask.

"Welcome, interlopers, whoever you are," said Fantômas. "Thank you for putting on the helms. Your swift, painful paralysis from the toxin contained within will now happen within seconds!"

What Fantômas did not know was that Lupin had, in secret, replaced the three red helms with harmless replicas. But suddenly he remembered . . . there were two black helms in the same room! He had not thought them significant but now he wondered, had they been poisoned? Had Fantômas pulled a final twist?

Lupin shouted, "Grognard, there were two black helms! Do you know what colour helm you are wearing?"

"No!" went the reply, and then suddenly his voice was muffled as he was tackled from behind.

Lupin shouted to Perceval the same question and he too did not know what colour his helm was, before the other monks grabbed him.

But now, with that information, Lupin knew which helm he wore.

Q: What colour is Lupin's helm, and how does he know?

Herlock Sholmes
and the Mona Lisas

T HE *MONA LISA* HAD been stolen! And who did they summon to
solve the crime but the world's greatest detective . . . Herlock
Sholmes! (Lupin insisted I refer to him as such . . .)

Sholmes and Doctor Wilson discussed the case during their voyage
to France.

"Could it be Lupin?" asked Wilson.

"No . . . Lupin loves the painting, but he would have no reason to
rob the Louvre. Get the captain to send a radio message to the museum;
they must put out a full-page advertisement in all popular newspapers,
offering a substantial reward to anyone who could come forward with
the stolen painting."

By the time Sholmes and Wilson had arrived in Paris, there was
already a small crowd of claimants around the entrance of the Louvre,
and the detective and his friend were ushered into the office of the
museum's director.

"I see the advertisement has had the appropriate effect," said Sholmes
wryly.

"Monsieur, they are a rabble of liars and opportunists, but I suspect
you knew that would be so," said the director, mopping his brow.

"And no sign of the painting?" asked Sholmes, filling his pipe idly.

"Oh no, sir, we've found the *Mona Lisa*," said the director bitterly. "In
fact, we have found three. Three people all claiming theirs is the true
painting."

The door was opened and two men and a woman entered, each
bearing what appeared to be the *Mona Lisa*. The men immediately began
barracking each other with accusations.

"My name is Louis Foncear, Monsieur Sholmes, and I know for a fact
that this man Alphonse Bonnay can only tell lies!"

"Pfft, be quiet, Louis!" said Alphonse. "I am no liar—it is this woman
next to me, Romain Babineux, who cannot tell the truth!"

"How dare you!" shouted Romain. "It is you two who are both liars,
you, you!"

"Well, following pure logic, there is only one answer," said Sholmes. "But following deductive reasoning, I suggest you choose whichever you feel looks most authentic . . ."

Q: a) Who, logically, has the true painting?
b) But then who, realistically, has the true painting?

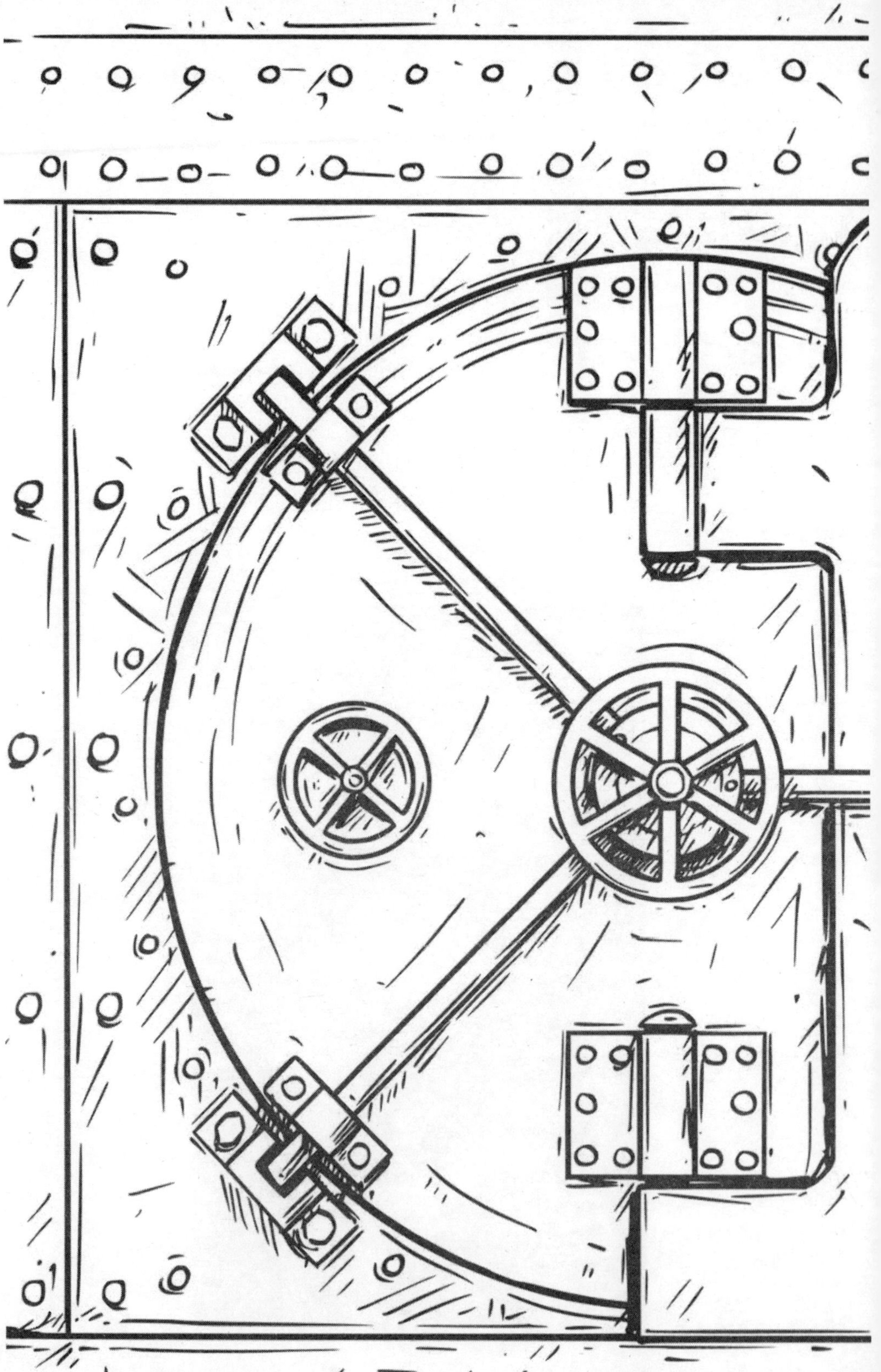

The Impregnable Vault

T HE MOBIUS SAFE THAT Lupin kept in his lair was not truly impregnable by him. He just chose not to open it. The only truly impregnable vault he ever faced was the one built for the financial genius Kilian König. He was known to have a head for numbers and very little else, in one incident even forgetting to wear trousers as he departed his house, but it was this ability that allowed him to predict the First World War and the stock market crash and consequently emerge as one of the richest men in the world. Why would he need to remember simple things like eating or when to go to bed when an army of servants could do all this for him? He needed only to think about numbers.

The only place König would not permit anyone else to go was the vault. It was constructed from steel-reinforced concrete inside an excavated mountain in an isolated part of the Alps. There was only one entrance, quintuple-locked with a system of locking bolts, pressure systems and rotation manifolds so complex it made Fort Knox seem a simple child's toy. The only key that opened it was surgically implanted in König's finger, and any attempt to remove or copy it would result in its destruction—as he discovered once when he forgot it was there and attempted to pick his nose and had to be rushed to surgery!

There was no way to get to the sides apart from drilling through an entire mountain, and any extreme vibration would trigger a dozen alarms. The 20 m thick vault door had copper lining that diffused any oxyacetylene torch. You could not even torture König to force him to open the safe (not that Lupin ever would), because his extreme absent-mindedness and number fixation made him immune to coercion, even through pain. Sometimes he did not even remember the vault's location!

No other person was permitted to go to the safe, König personally moving any money or items back and forth himself. Unlike a bank where people could be bribed or corrupted, this single man was the only one who could unlock or lock the vault.

And yet, despite all this, one fateful day Lupin stole every single thing in the vault, and it was the easiest thing he had ever done!

Q: *How could Lupin steal everything from this impregnable vault?*

The Strange Device

L UPIN HAD NOT THOUGHT Liseron would go so far. In the interven-
ing weeks his doppelganger had committed ever more audacious
robberies and the whole of France was abuzz about this new rival for
Lupin's crown. But there was something about the crimes that had not
seemed right to him. Finally, when he had looked at their planning and
timing he began to suspect they were being used to distract and draw
the police and public's attention from some other, stranger plan, and
his suspicions were confirmed when the body of Le Troglodiste washed
up in the Paris river . . . drowned. How could a man whose life was lived
mostly underwater drown?

Lupin drew on all his contacts and now found himself here, deep
within the catacombs, in a place where even the Phantom of the Opera
would baulk to go. Squatting in a chamber was an immense device with
steel tendrils reaching all throughout the underside of Paris, pumping
something into the water supply. Lupin held his lantern higher and tried
to read the dials. It seemed there were twelve primary pumps, and collectively they were pumping 12 litres of this substance into the water every
12 minutes. One by one he managed to shut them down, until only one
remained, but he could not stop it. At least, he reasoned, whatever it was
doing would be considerably slowed.

Q: *If twelve pumps can pump 12 litres into the water every 12 minutes,
how long will it take one pump to pump 1 litre?*

Who is Liseron?

L UPIN GOT A CHEMIST friend of his to examine the fluid. They said that within the capabilities of their understanding it seemed to be simply water, although they did find mild traces of ergot fungus.

It was time for Lupin to learn who Liseron was; he had dallied for too long thinking this weed was not a threat to him, when plainly they were a threat to the whole of France. Their influence had grown, fed by the sunlight of publicity.

Whoever they were, they were extremely clever, especially in the sciences. They had skills at observation and mimicry. They could make themselves seem unobtrusive and harmless, but in reality they were carnivorous, devouring his life, his reputation. They sought to conquer, like the Romans of old, speaking with sophisticated words in Latin but acting with ferocious barbarity. And they knew how to bait a trap and lure people in by appearing to be what they were not.

Q: *Who is Liseron? Look back over the previous puzzles and find the one person who matches the description Lupin gives. There is an extra clue in the solution of the puzzle they are in, which spells the word "LISERON."*

NOTE:
SOLVE THIS PUZZLE BEFORE YOU READ THE NEXT PAGE

The Capture of Liseron

G ANIMARD COULD NOT BELIEVE his eyes! Lupin had messaged him, asked him to assemble all the press, and now here standing before him in the largest room in the police préfecture, in front of dozens of reporters and policemen, was Lupin himself!

Lupin wore a large loose-fitting cloak and was clutching his throat. He looked very drawn and thin, his body strangely bulky, but he had the arrogant stance and keen intelligent eyes Ganimard recognized. Kneeling before him, a pistol to her head, was a woman in chains with wild, angry eyes and thick makeup.

"Meet Liseron, AKA Geneviève de Barre," said Lupin croakily. "Rogue botanist attempting to poison Paris. I found her machine."

"You did not destroy it, I trust?" the woman spat, glaring at him. "No, you could not! Not Lupin, the 20th-century made flesh, the industrial revolutionary! I hated having to use a machine to achieve my aims, but the plants can only do so much . . ."

"Tell us all your aims!" declaimed Lupin, pushing her forward.

"France is sick!" she cried to the journalists. "We have moved too far from nature and the land toward mechanization and technology! Arsène Lupin is but a symptom of our sickness, the modern thief with modern gadgets, plundering our past! But there is another way!"

The journalists ferociously wrote this down.

"We can . . . we can . . ." the woman faltered.

"You want to smash all the machinery, don't you?" said Lupin hoarsely, prodding her with his gun, a piece of paper falling from it next to the woman.

"Yes, that is right. Soon all of France will be able to breathe the sweet summer air, free from smoke and fumes! Just imagine it! Breathe deeply and imagine!"

Something was wrong. Ganimard had to signal to the police to seize Liseron and Lupin immediately, but they seemed strangely interested in her strong words and the strangely sweet scent. Then he thought he saw Le Troglodiste, the gas mask-wearing underdweller, enter the room!

"Men . . . seize Liseron and Lupin . . ." he said, his words strangely slurred.

Q: *Who should the police seize if they wish to capture*
a) Liseron and b) Lupin?

The Death of Lupin

LUPIN HAD TO GIVE her credit. Liseron must have realized Lupin would discover her identity and so instead seized the initiative, using the situation to propagate her anti-technology manifesto and gas them with some kind of hypnotic drug. It's not exactly what he would have done, but you had to admire her flair!

Lupin had come straight from the site of her machine, where he had a few trusted friends dismantling it. The liquid within contained some kind of lysergic acid compound, designed to soften the minds of the Parisian people. He'd stopped that, but if she could control the brains of the press and the police, then the public would soon follow.

Liseron, dressed as Lupin, turned to look at Lupin dressed as Le Troglodiste (a hasty last-minute protection against the gas) and smiled bitterly. "Oh look, the world's greatest thief, here to steal my moment!"

"Your moment? You're dressed as me!" said Lupin incredulously, moving toward her.

"I'm sorry, I can't hear you!" said Liseron, pulling out a pistol. "Remove the mask, it's muffling your voice . . ."

"I suppose a pistol doesn't count as a modern invention," said Lupin wryly.

"It's an antique," she said, "Gentlemen, seize this creature."

The assembled group lurched sleepily toward Lupin.

"You see, the gas makes them suggestible. They do what you tell them, and say what you want them to say!" Liseron crowed triumphantly, cocking her gun.

Lupin had but moments to act. He turned to Ganimard.

"When this is done, you will be standing over my dead body, but it is the right thing to do for this country!"

And with that he lunged at Liseron, their bodies meeting as the gun exploded in her hand. She fell to the ground, a grievous wound in her chest, and Lupin fell alongside her, not moving. Ganimard knelt down and felt Lupin's pulse.

"Lupin is dead," he intoned monotonously.

The body was quickly taken away, and no ceremony was conducted or corpse interred, as France refused to revere such a criminal. But France collectively mourned the loss of the king of thieves and the thief of kings. Lupin was dead.

Q: . . . Is Lupin really dead?

Fin

Solutions

Page 10
THE SUNSET RUBY

The police commissary is Arsène Lupin. The others cannot be him because the old woman's wrinkles are real, the soldier only has one eye, the small man is genuinely small and the Pantaloon actor has a real hooked nose.

We also learn that: a) there was formerly a man in an overcoat in the room; b) there is a discarded overcoat on the floor; c) there is a man-sized sculpture in the corner; d) the commissary has chalky whiteness on his neck; and e) the Pantaloon clown's makeup looks poorly applied.

Lupin entered the room dressed as Pantaloon, stole the ruby, and in the chaos ducked behind the sculpture and changed clothes with the hooked-nose man in the overcoat, a confederate of his, putting on the commissary uniform concealed underneath and wiping off his makeup while the accomplice hastily applied his own makeup. He then stepped forward immediately as the room opened, taking charge. Unfortunately he has just slipped out behind you.

Page 13
THE STAINED GLASS WINDOWS

The Rodin bronze is 26 kg.
The Sormani ormolu-mounted table is 3 kg less, so is 23 kg.
The Roman statue of Venus is 23 x 2 + 1 = 47 kg.
The solid gold tureen must be 26 + 10 ÷ 2, which is 18 kg.
The commode is 18 - 2, which is 16 kg.

To balance the scaffold you must have the statue and tureen on one side (47 + 18 = 65 kg), and the bronze, table and commode on the other (26 + 23 + 16 = 65 kg).

You also realize that as he was telling you this tale, Lupin has stolen your watch.

Page 14
THE SOCIETY OF BLANC ET NOIR

Lupin pulled out three gloves, thereby guaranteeing that at least two of the gloves would either be black or white.

Page 15

THE PROBLEM WITH COFFEE AND COMFORT?

100 x 2 is 200 DM for all the chairs.

10 x 52 = 520, so he was spending 520 DM a year on coffee.

5 x 52 = 260, so he saved 260 DM by switching to the cheaper coffee.

200 x 10= 2,000, so he was getting 2,000 pfennigs a day from coffee. There are 100 pfennigs in a DM, so that is 20 DM.

80 percent of 20 DM is 16 DM, so the profit lost was 4 DM a day.

4 x 365 = 1,460 DM lost in a year.

If you subtract the chair cost and the coffee savings from the lost coffee sales, 1460 - 200 - 260 = 1,000, so switching coffee has led to a loss of 1,000 DM and therefore was not the correct decision.

Page 16

A BREATH-TAKING INTERACTION IN MADRID

Gutiérrez explained that Liseron, the false Lupin, burned through the steel bars with nitric acid, causing the streaks of liquid metal. The guard was already asleep, as evidenced by his pillow, and Liseron had intended to steal the coins without waking him. But the acid had dripped onto the marble statue, causing the damage. Acid on marble releases carbon dioxide, which has no scent, so once Liseron had departed, the room filled with this gas, knocking the guard out and causing nausea and confusion.

Page 18

THE BOOKS OF DOCTOR PECQUEUX

Its pages were made of paper, not vellum, and paper books were a much later development than 1543. Vellum was made from calfskin stretched and treated, and therefore would have different colours on the inside and outside of the skin, plus evidence of hair follicles from the animal. Vellum is also heavier than paper, so the book is too light, and paper absorbs ink, as Lupin demonstrates with the bottle.

Page 20

THE MYSTERIOUS SECRET OF BOUILLABAISSE

a) On Monday they caught sea urchins and crab, on Tuesday they caught John Dory and weeverfish, on Wednesday they caught lobster and mussels, and on Thursday they caught red gurnard and monkfish.

b) The bouillabaise was therefore made by Albain Descouteux on Thursday, and he was soon arrested for the theft.

Page 23

THE ART OF THE STEEL

Mr. Finch was responsible. A goose had nested in the coke oven, and he'd closed it down because he loved animals and wanted to protect them. The rusty gate/horn noise they heard was a goose honk, and the feathers in Finch's pockets were from there too. As they approached the oven, Finch threw his wrench behind them and then claimed to have seen the running man. Bryant (Lupin) had realized this and spoke up, referencing geese and eggs to show Finch he understood and to give him a chance to move the nest.

Page 24

LE BOURGET ROBBERY PART I—THE VANISHING GOLD

They melted the gold sovereigns in the bread oven. 2,000 °F is much too high to cook bread, but gold melts at 1,948 °F. Then they poured it into casts that they stole from the foundry, painted them with the greyish lead paint to look like iron, and installed them on the old woman's windows, planning to return when the heat had died down and take them away again.

Page 26

THE LIGHTNING THIEF

24 is 3 x 8, so an 8 FPS film must go through 3 times as slow. 456 ÷ 3 = 152 mm a second. The film was 3 minutes long, so 180 seconds, and 180 x 152 = 27,360 mm or 27.36 m.

Page 27

LE BOURGET ROBBERY PART II—THE OBVIOUS SUSPECT

Idette liked to go to Parc Montsouris (whose name comes from "mocking mice" in French) to feed the pigeons or "Carriers of Hope," as they were called during the siege of Paris in 1870. Some men tried to rob her, but Bret scared them off with his broom. She brought him back to her house and, knowing he liked art, gave him a painting of Oberon and Titania she had inherited. He took it to an art dealer who recognized it as *The Fairy Lovers* by Theodor von Holst and paid Bret for it, although it was much less than it was worth. Lupin told the art dealer to come clean and give Bret and Madame Perrault its true value, and they moved into a bigger house together and lived happily ever after.

Page 28

RIDDLE OF THE DANCING SEAGULL

Seagulls dance (stamp their feet rhythmically) to imitate the sound of rain on the beach, which draws worms to the surface to eat. Worms come to the surface when they think it is raining because they move faster through wet sand or soil.

Page 30

THE FOUR ROOMS OF FELICITE LEFLEUVE

The sword in the Duchamp room is the best chance. Gropius is sober and watching the bowl. Picasso is literally holding and using the puzzle box. And Hopper is carefully studying everyone's faces. Duchamp, however, is playing chess, doesn't care about the sword and doesn't care about lawbreakers either.

Page 32

THE CHAGRIN OF CHEZ DARIEN

20 percent off 44 = 35.20.
20 percent off 35.20 = 28.16.
20 percent off 28.16 = 22.528.
So only twice, actually.

Page 33

THE TOMB OF ROBERT D'ARGENT

The mother of Uriel is Terese, the mother of Quentin is Plaisance, and the father of Sylvie is Robert. This means that Terese is Plaisance's sister and Robert is Plaisance's brother. So, Uriel, Quentin and Sylvie are cousins. The bracelet was split between them.

Page 35

NAPOLEON'S SWORD

Gare d'Austerliz. Napoleon had a great victory at Austerlitz in 1805, whereas he faced great defeat at Waterloo in 1815. King's Cross, funnily enough, is considered to be the site of Boudica's final battle . . .

Page 36

LE BOURGET ROBBERY PART III—THE BETRAYAL

Tasse attacked the guard, and Fournier stole the gold.

Tasse is Catholic, hence the rosary beads, and after depositing the gold he went to Sacré-Coeur to confess to a priest about attacking

the guard, who could not reveal that he was there due to the sanctity of the confessional.

Morel was not in a bar but under the Pont Neuf, which has a series of "mascarons," stone masks that were the ashen horned faces he saw.

Fournier says he could not stand the sight of blood. However, the Grand Guignol theatre is notorious for its gory content so he could not have been there. Instead, he faked the robbery of his shop, but smashed all the windows when he only needed to break one. Lupin informed the police of this and considered adding a priest costume to his wardrobe.

Page 38
LUPIN ESCAPES THE BOARS
Lupin used the locations and the news reporting to send an acronym to his ally. Lille, Ypres, Orléans and Nice spells LYON!

Page 39
THE DEATH OF FRANS SONNE
Mercury. The first planet from the sun is Mercury; it was the liquid metal Mercury from the thermometer that fell on the coals and released its toxic fumes; and Hermès is the original Greek version of Mercury, the winged messenger from Roman mythology.

Page 40
THE FUSES OF LAS FALLAS
As the fuses burn inconsistently, simply lighting one and waiting until it's three quarters gone would not work. Instead, Lupin lit the first fuse at both ends, knowing it would take 30 minutes, and lit the other at one end. Once the first fuse was used up, he lit the other end of the second fuse. As that had already burned for 30 minutes, it would only have 30 minutes left and lighting it at both ends then meant it would now take 15 minutes, allowing him to measure 45 minutes.

Page 41
BUREAU DE CHANGE
The answer is 2, because multiplying and adding give the same answer:

$2 \times 2 = 4$.

$2 + 2 = 4$.

Page 43

THE FIVE KNIGHTS

Armand de Blanc. Mimosas are yellow, oranges grow from a seed, green indicates envy and greed, indigo is a dye used in India and China, the violet grows in February in Toulouse, and blood is red. Combining all colours together in the light spectrum gives white light.

Page 44

THE COUNTESS'S CONUNDRUM

Lupin can say: c) "You will gut me like a salmon." This cannot be true, as a truth will lead to him being thrown off the train. But it cannot be a lie, as if he lies, she will do the very thing he has just said. Therefore, she would be forced to release him.

a) can be said to be a lie.

b) can be said to be the truth.

c) will confound her as it is neither the truth nor a lie.

Page 45

THE PÉTANQUE WAGER

Ten rounds. Lupin must have won two rounds, so to be 18 francs up the millionaire must have played two other games, and then six further ones (6 x 3 = 18).

Page 47

THE CALENDAR BRIDGE

The path was indicated by the number of letters in the name of each month. The numbers were 9 (Septembre), 4 (Juin), 3 (Mai), 5 (Avril), 7, 7 (Fevrier twice) and 8 (Décembre).

Page 48

ROULETTE OF THE RUSSIAN

Yes, Lupin will have a better chance if he spins the chambers. One bullet in six chambers gave him a 1 in 6 chance. After the trigger was pulled, that gives a 1 in 5 chance. But if he spins again, it returns to being a 1 in 6 chance.

Page 49

THE TALE OF LECANARD

The four values of the coins are 1, 2, 5 and 8.

1 + 2 = 3, 2 + 2 = 4, 5 + 1 = 6, 5 + 2 = 7, 8 + 1 = 9, and 8 + 2 = 10.

Page 50

THE IMPOSSIBLE LEAP

Lupin didn't leap off the balcony. He bribed Anton with the gold sovereigns (to cover his gambling debts) and quickly gave him the story to tell, then he hid behind the new velvet curtains.

Page 52

THE WALL OF THESEUS

3,873,000,000 x 7 = 27,111,000,000 hours.

8,760 hours in a year. 27,111,000,000 ÷ 8,760 = 3,094,863 years.

3,873,000,000 ÷ 5,000 = 774,600.

774,600 x 2 = 1,549,200 days waiting for bricks to be made.

365 days in a year. 1,549,200 ÷ 365 = 4,244 years.

So it takes 3,094,863 + 4,244 = 3,099,107 years to replace all the bricks!

Page 55

THE TORMENT MACHINE OF BARON VON DER LEYEN UND ZU HOHENGEROLDSECK

Box b) "FAKE" has the real rubies. If *every* box is mislabelled, then a fake ruby from a box marked "BOTH" means it must be the box of fakes. Therefore, box b) must be the real rubies because it is marked "FAKE," and if it were both that would mean box a) "REAL" was marked correctly—which we know isn't the case.

Page 56

THE SHATTERED GLASS

Lupin fed dirt through the ventilation system into the bottle, then a single potato plant seed, and then dripped water onto it. Over time the potato grew, and once it was too big for the bottle, it smashed. Then when Lupin entered as the insurance agent, he took the statue from where it had fallen behind the podium and grabbed the potato, pretending it was an apple.

Page 58

THE CHURCH CLOCK

Louvel Danieu. The times represent directions. When it's AM you move in the direction of the hour hand, and PM the minute hand. Starting at Evonne Bellerose, you go up, up, left, left, up, up and left, to reach Louvel Danieu's grave.

Page 59

THE DEADLY JAR

It was honey—hence the hexagonal shape, like a beehive. Honey is naturally antibiotic and can survive for a long time without developing fungus or other germs dangerous to humans.

Page 61

THE HAIR OF MÉLUSINE

He was stung by an Irukandji jellyfish, the venom of which causes Irukandji syndrome, characterized by sweating, anxiety and a feeling of despair. The only treatment is vinegar for the stings and then an analgesic such as morphine.

Page 62

THE VANISHING FRANC

There is no missing franc. The fact remains that there are 25 francs in the till at the restaurant, 2 francs in the kitchen boy's hand and 1 franc each given to Hilbert's friends, making 30.

9 + 9 + 9 is not an amount they *did* pay, only what they could have paid, and the 2 francs the kitchen boy kept would be part of that total.

Page 63

CHATON'S HORDE

It is the number of HANDS, FEET, TAILS, EYES and TOES that both Chaton and Brujon have.

Chaton lost a hand and two toes, so the first half of the code is 1, 2, 0, 2, 8. Brujon lost an eye and cats have 18 toes (this is why the dial can go up to 20). Brujon is also a Manx cat and therefore has no tail! So, the second half of the code is 0, 4, 0, 1, 18.

Page 64

THE FUNERAL OF SIMON DE SAUTER

Castelmary earned 120, the largest amount. Verlaine earned 40, a third of 120. Permont earned 80, double Verlaine's amount. Jehan Pelletier earned as much as Ardout and Verlaine combined, so it must be 70 as that is 40 and 30 combined, and therefore Ardout earned 30.

Page 66
THE BOUNCING BALL

Theoretically an infinite number of times, because any number can be divided in half infinitely. In reality gravity would cause it to slow and stop, and without any other variables it's not possible to say when this would be.

Page 68
THE TIDES OF BINIC

The Aigrette was a submarine and was currently submerged. This is why sometimes Lupin could not see it despite his clear vantage point, and also why its surface was so strongly sealed.

Page 69
THE DISAPPEARING FRIEND

If the man telling Lupin the story had never seen or heard about his friend from the moment they jumped, it's not possible for him to know his friend became tangled in a tree and broke his neck.

Page 70
THE STRANGE CREATURE

A jug. It has a neck, lip, mouth and bottom, with a design of a face on it, and it's made of bone china.

Page 71
THE DIABOLICAL DOOR CODE

The number reply in each case was not half the number, as the fake Lupin presumed, but actually the number of letters in each word ("six" has three letters, "twelve" has six). So, he should have replied, "Five."

Page 73
THE RIDDLE OF THE CLOCK

During daylight saving time, when the time is moved back an hour, the clock will read correctly for a third time. This was first introduced in Port Arthur, Ontario, Canada, in 1908.

Page 74
THE FALLING KEY

In his previous visit to the castle, Lupin froze the key in a block of ice and placed it in the grille above the cell. He knew the weather was due to get warmer, melting it and allowing the key to drop through the grille's holes.

Page 77
THE CAUGHT JESTER
It was a costume from when the actor played the Fool in *King Lear*, kept as a memento. Lupin used too much dynamite and burnt the clothes he was wearing by accident (the scraps of cloth), and the only alternative was the costume on the mannequin.

Page 78
THE HONESTY OF HENRI
"Yes." That is a truthful one-word response to the question, "Is it head or tails?" (Any other positive one-word affirmation is also acceptable.)

Page 79
THE CARDINAL DIRECTIONS
The sun sets in the west, and as the setting sun's light was coming through the front or helm of the boat, that means they were heading west toward Blangy-sur-Bresle.

Page 80
THE INSURMOUNTABLE NUMBER
9 7 8 0 1 1. "The head and the tail come first" means you use the first and last numbers. "Other numbers are not even relevant, unless they are the same when you stand on your head" means you discount any even numbers unless they are the same upside down, such as 8 and 0. "Then the last two are strangely the same" means the two odd (strange) numbers are the same, both 1.

Page 81
THE EGGS OF FABERGÉ
Seven. The first collaborator took 3.5 eggs (half of 7) and half an egg (0.5), adding up to 4, leaving 3 eggs. The second collaborator took 1.5 eggs (half of 3) and half an egg (0.5), adding up to 2, leaving the final egg for Lupin.

Page 83
THE DESCENSO DEL DIABLO
He would need 55 - (3 + 1.79 + 0.65) + 3 x 2 = 55.56 m of rope.

Page 84
THE BALLAD OF POOR JEAN
Monsieur Charbonneau is in fact quite wealthy but hoards his money, a cache of gold sovereigns, in the room he does not visit, only spending it occasionally. This is why he is not ill-nourished, has a hat made of vicuña wool (the most expensive fabric in the world), does not have holes in his shoes, unlike most of his neighbours, has caviar (the black eggs), and has a bottle of 1846 Meursault Charmes, a very valuable bottle of wine.

Page 86
THE HISTORY OF L'HISTOIRE DE CARDENIO
1) It should not be in French as Shakespeare's plays were not translated into other languages until after his death. The first French translation of his work was by Pierre-Antoine de La Place in 1745.
2) The Taj Mahal was not commissioned until 1632, and not completed until 1653.
3) Barometers were not invented until 1640 at the earliest.
4) Sparkling champagne was not created until 1662.
5) The First Folio of Shakespeare's plays was released by John Heminges and Henry Condell in 1623.

Page 89
THE TRUFFLE PIG
She was mated with Bucephalus the boar to produce a "litter" of piglets. This is why she was gone for 120 days (the normal pig gestation period), and why Lupin made reference to children and baptism.

Page 90
THE FATEFUL DATE OF ROBESPIERRE
The 13th of Fructidor.

Page 92
SYLVIE'S BELOVED
Because he was a horse, specifically a Camargue horse. These are an ancient breed, with many living wild, and they always have long grey manes. Horses are muscular, run fast, have long noses and are herbivores.

Page 93
THE FALL OF MARIANNE
Because he made his body straight and entered feet first. Edgard hit the water on his back with his arms out, maximizing his surface area. The boat driver thought that the statue had broken the water's surface, making it less impactful for Lupin, but that is actually a myth.

Page 95
THE CHEESE VAULTS OF BASSOUES
At the first crossroads he went right, as that was the Camembert and left was some Reblochon. At the second he went ahead, as that was the Roquefort, with Camembert on the left and Emmenthal on the right. Then at the end he went left, as that was more Emmenthal, with Comté on the right.

Page 96
THE VILLAINOUS VINEYARD
Because red grapes such as Pinot Noir are often used to make sparkling white wines like champagne. They press them carefully to ensure the juice is not coloured.

Page 97
THE TIFLIS RAID
Kamo was released because his sentences were commuted, and then in 1917 the October Revolution happened, and his fellow Bolshevik robbers became high-ranking Soviet officials. One of them was Lenin himself, and Erivansky Square was renamed Lenin Square in 1921. Another was Joseph Stalin, notoriously responsible for many executions, secret murders and deadly economic policies.

Page 99
PARIS EXPOSITION
The mirrors from the Palace of Optics' kaleidoscope.

Page 100
THE TIME OF RELEASE
Only one month. "The month before two months after" means only one month before. "The month before next month" would be the month they are in now. So if that month is July, then they are in June and he has only one month until release.

Page 101
THE BARREL OF NAPOLEON
By tipping the barrel to its side so that the brandy is slightly touching the lip. If you can see the barrel's bottom, then it's less than half full, but if the bottom still can't be seen, then it is more.

Page 102
THE MYSTERIOUS MEAL
Snails, which have a single "muscular ventral foot" on the bottom of their body that they ripple to move along.

Page 103
THE UNWANTED DELIVERY
Lupin stole a lion from the Ménagerie du Jardin des plantes—a zoo in Versailles. There is a lion on the heraldic flag of Lyon. However, DeHeliot wanted the lion to be in one of his cages, not in his bedroom!

Page 105
THE VISITING CARD
He thinks the Duke staged the robbery of his house after receiving the card from Lupin so that he could save his items from theft but claim on the insurance. The card said Lupin would visit on the Ides, which is the 15th of March, but the items were stolen the night of the 13th. Lupin said he would carefully, cleanly remove the items, as he could with his famed skills, but the drag marks and dents suggest a clumsy robbery. The two guards were rubbing their arms and necks from all the heavy lifting they had had to do. Furthermore, the glass on the lawn indicated the window had been broken from the inside, not the outside.

Page 106
THE BELLS OF NOTRE DAME
Lupin did not ring one of the Notre Dame bells but a small handbell he had in his pocket, which caused the trained bird in his sack (his ally) to attack Le Style.

Page 109
THE BEHEADING GAME
The mayor beheaded it himself.

Page 110

THE REVOLUTIONARY CAKE

Humans need 2,000 calories; one slice of cake has 250, so humans need eight slices of cake per day. The population of France was 28 million and cakes have 12 slices, so 8 x 28,000,000 ÷ 12 = 18,666,666.67 cakes per day.

Page 111

ALL FOR ONE

It is Porthos (Port is the wine in his name).

Page 112

THE PRISONER'S DILEMMA

Lupin and Mr. H were in fact the same man! When Lupin was captured, he escaped using the tunnels and was then captured as Mr. H. He then moved between the cells as necessary, relying on the darkness and the limited interaction with the guards.

Page 114

THE EIFFEL CONUNDRUM

Yes.

Page 115

THE SECRET OF THE APARTMENT

The Statue of Liberty, an iconic statue made of copper. Its inner structural work was designed by Eiffel's company, and then they built the statue itself.

Page 116

LUPIN VS GUSTAVE EIFFEL

Lupin used a parachute that Eiffel was keeping for safety purposes. This was the folded silk item that Lupin spotted. Prototypes had been developed by Franz Reichelt and a dummy was apparently dropped from the tower in 1911 (although we now know otherwise). Sadly, Reichelt himself died jumping from the tower in a test in 1912.

Page 117

THE RIDDLE OF THE FIRES

He was in a bar. The animal skin was leather or suede, and the dried worm fluids were silk. The rancid potato juice was vodka. The banging of drums was a live band, and the lit fires were cigarettes, cigars or pipes.

Page 118

RIDDLE OF THE CHIMERA

A duck-billed platypus. These animals have a duck-like bill (obviously), dense mole-like fur, a broad flat tail, electroreceptive senses like an elephant fish or dolphin, and a spur on their hind feet that can deliver a venom that is painful and potentially paralyzing to humans.

Page 120

THE HORRIFYING ATTACK

Because it was only about a damaged book, in this case *Louis Lambert* by Balzac. The book's spine had been broken and pages (or leaves) torn out by the four-year-old boy, including the book's appendix, plus there was dirt on the dust jacket. Therefore, it was only good for bookworms.

Page 121

THE FIVE ASSASSINS

Acelin gets drunk, Bartholomew fears dogs, Cornélie has a gambling problem, Fitz hates bright light, and Emile is afraid of the dark.

Page 122

THE PANAMA GUZZLER

a) Rex Passineli is the odd one out, as it is not an anagram of Arsène Lupin.

b) The letters absent from Rex Passineli that are present in Arsène Lupin are U and N, which spell "un," masculine French for "one". Instead, it has the letters S, I and X, which spells "six." Therefore, you swap the 1s in the code for 6s and get 6 6 6 8 6 5 9 6.

Page 125

LUPIN'S CREED

Yes, because it doesn't matter what weight you are—any increase in weight and therefore gravitational force cancels each other out by a decrease in acceleration.

Page 126

THE SIX WIVES OF HARRY BUTLER JR

Wives number one, three and six were the same woman, who was the same age as Harry because they were at school together. She's 45.
Wife number two is in her thirties, so younger than Harry.
Wife number four is in her early twenties, so is the youngest.

Wife number five is older than Harry, so got the most.
So wife number five got $30,000.
Wife number two got $15,000.
Therefore wife number one, three and *six* got $7,500!

Page 128
THE FABULOUS OBJECTS

They are all constellations of stars (glittering in a dark room).
Antlia—air pump, Horologium—pendulum clock, Libra—scales, Pictor—easel, Fornax—chemical furnace, Crater—cup, Lyra—lyre/harp, Octans—octant, Pyxis—compass (for people at sea), Scutum—shield, Sextans—sextant, Telescopium—telescope, Ursa Major— great bear, incorporating the Plough constellation, and Ursa Minor—little bear.

Page 129
THE BODY OF ARSÈNE LUPIN

Because it was a museum dummy made to look like Lupin! Its body was stiff because it was made of wood and the limbs had just fallen off, the glassy fixed expression was its face and the clothes were replicas. Lupin had broken into the museum, stolen the dummy and slung it in the Seine in disgust.

Page 131
THE HAUL OF LE TROGLODISTE

3 diamonds, 4 sapphires, 2 rubies and 5 emeralds. There are four types of jewels. We know that all but 11 are diamonds, so, there must be 11 sapphires, rubies and emeralds total. Using this information, we can make similar eliminations for the other jewel types allowing us to calculate how many of each Le Troglodiste has acquired.

Page 132
THE FOOLISH ROBBERS

Because it is gazpacho, an Andalusian vegetable soup served ice cold, traditionally made in a mortar and pestle and then cooled in an earthenware pot.

Page 133
THE FATEFUL FOOTPRINTS

Because the rising sun will melt the snow, especially as it's growing warmer, and no footprints will be visible

Page 134
THE MÈRE DE LUPIN
If Lupin's father died a year before Lupin's birth, he could not have conceived him. Furthermore, she claimed to have no family, then claimed to have a sister. If she was truly 41, then as the year is 1908 she must have had Lupin when she was six years old.

Page 135
THE FORCES OF FANTÔMAS
332 monks. Here are the calculations, working backward from the monk's answer: 250 - 1 = 249. 249 x 8 = 1,992. 1,992 ÷ 2 = 996. 996 x 4 = 3,984. 3,984 ÷ 3 = 1,328. 1,328 ÷ 4 = 332.

Page 137
THE SUSPICIONS OF MONSIEUR LUPIN
The second, as "Julius Monisse-Seronier" is an anagram of "Je suis Monsieur Liseron."

Page 138
THE POISONED CUP
a) From left to right they are Pertwee, Brockhurst and Finsdale, as Finsdale ends up with the chalice at the end of the line, and Brockhurst is Finsdale's "right-hand man" and sits to his right—which is our left.
b) Ultimately Pertwee has the chalice, Brockhurst the vessel, and Finsdale the flagon.

Page 141
THE RIDDLE OF THE CASTLE
It refers to the hearts and blood of the many generations of *rats* that have lived in the castle for over a hundred years.

Page 142
THE GAULISH POTION
a) Blue berries make you strong but make you double in size. Yellow berries make you tough but slow you down by four times. Red berries make you twice as fast but make you shrink four times smaller than usual.
b) A potion with four blue berries, one yellow berry and two red berries will create the desired effect. The four blue berries counteract the shrinking effect of the red berries, and the two red berries counteract the slowing effect of the yellow berry.

Page 143
LUPIN'S CELL
They are Roman numerals. I = 1, V = 5, X = 10 etc.

Page 145
THE MRACULOUS WALK
Because it had frozen in the winter cold. The officer who tried to pursue him was too big and fell through the ice.

Page 146
THE HOUSE OF THE NEMESIS
Number 11. Hilbert considers *himself* to be his own worst enemy.

Page 147
ROCHAMBORD'S BIRTHDAY GIFT
He is his own step-grandfather. As the Comte married his mother and Rochambord married the Comte's mother, that makes the two mothers each other's step-mothers, but it also means that as the Comte's mother is stepmother to Rochambord's mother, she is Rochambord's step-grandmother, and therefore he is his own step-grandfather.

Page 149
THE SOCIALIST HIGHWAYMAN
The Count gave 25 francs to Denis Moreau (remember, it must be shared amongst all five people there), and then 10 francs to the carriage driver. Then the Count's daughter broke a charm off her bracelet (worth 5 francs) and gave that to the carriage driver. Now Denis Moreau has 25 silver francs, the Count has 25 silver francs, the daughter has five charms worth 25 francs, and the carriage driver has 10 franc coins, a 5 franc charm and the 10 franc watch, adding up to 25 francs.

Page 150
THE PALE WORKMAN
He is a grave-digger who works at night. He doesn't wear a cloak because it might make people think he is a ghost or the grim reaper, he does much digging and hauling of coffins, and the people around him are dead people in their graves, with their names set in stone on their tombs. He's eating a croissant because he is just beginning his day.

Page 151

THE MOBIUS SAFE

No. Any number progression you follow—because it involves multiplying by 2—will inevitably become an even number, at which point it is impossible to reach the odd number of 1. (If the dial had 21 numbers on it, you could go 1, 2, 4, 8, 16, 11, 1.)

Page 152

THE MUSEUM MYSTERY

Lupin is pretending to be the mannequin of Foucault. It is not meant to be there and does not look like him.

Page 155

THE COMPASS IN THE COURTYARD

Lupin ran west, north-east, west, north, east, north-west, north, east, west and north-east, which, using the initials of the French cardinal directions (in which "West" is "Ouest"), spells out ONE, ONE, NONE, ONE, indicating he had to set the first, second and fourth levers to 1.

Page 156

THE FENCING MATCHES

a) The pattern is DeSmet-Von Blyenburgh-Stuyck on the left-hand side, and Frelupt-DeSmet-DeSchepper-Stuyck on the right.

b) The tenth bout would have to be DeSmet vs DeSmet, which is impossible (unless he had a brother or other relative!).

Page 158

THE ENORMOUS DARKNESS

The planet Earth, when it blocks the Sun and its shadow falls on the Moon. During a lunar eclipse it blocks the Moon entirely and causes "darkness to fall upon itself."

Page 159

THE GO-BETWEEN

24 km. If the two groups are 8 km apart and both are moving toward each other at 4 kph, then it will take them an hour to meet in the middle. Therefore Moreau was going back and forth at 24 km per hour for an hour.

Page 160
THE MYSTERY OF THE LEGIONNAIRES

Jacques was the carpenter: his fingers are stained from furniture polish, his hair has sawdust in it and he keeps pencils behind his ear, as is common.

Pierre was the coal miner, as he still has traces of coal dust on his eyes and under his nails, and is unaccustomed to being above ground and in the light.

Alphonse was a dancer; his strong leg muscles allow him to run fast, and his love of dancing and rhythm causes him to tap his foot when at rest.

Françoise was a tennis player, as demonstrated by his tendency to sway from side to side as if preparing for a volley, as well as having a much more muscular right arm from using the racket.

René was the sailor, as he has a weather-beaten face, is covered in tattoos that he tries to hide, and has the side-to-side gait of someone who has worked on boats for long periods of time.

Page 163
THE BIZARRE ROBBERY

The first three objects they name have the same first letter of the name of the person who next speaks. Then the first letter of the second three objects they name is the same as the second letter of the name of the person who next speaks. Then the third, and so on.

Page 164
THE BIRTHDAY GOLD

Marguerite was born on the 29th of February in a leap year. Therefore she only actually had a birthday 19 times (76 divided by 4) and deposited 19,000 francs. Gina, however, was not, and had 56 birthdays, and as 56 x 300 = 16,800, that meant that there was only 2,200 francs left by 1912.

Page 165
THE UNWANTED VISITOR

Because the woman is not staying in the boarding house, but in fact lives next door at Number 2 rue du Chevalier-de-La-Barre. It's unlikely the man thought a completely different house was his boarding-house room.

Page 166
THE FAILING MONTGOLFIÈRE

Lupin and the rope. None of the objects are heavy enough in combination to allow the balloon to begin rising, so his best chance of escape is to use the rope to jump the seven yards to the ground, and take advantage of the element of surprise to run away.

Page 167
THE PEARL OF ISCHIA

It's a champion racing greyhound. He has white glossy fur, is bred rather than wild, and the greyhound racing track is shaped like an oval.

Page 168
THE VENETIAN ESCAPE

He didn't actually drive the car, but merely hid inside. It was a prop car used to promote the *Keystone Cops* film. Once he was inside, he hid and waited for the crowd to disperse.

Page 170
THE FOUNTAIN OF YOUTH

Nikolaos was born in 1945 BC, so he would be 35 in 1910 BC and 45 in 1900 BC, ten years later.

Page 171
THE FORTUNATE GALLERY

The artist has died.

Page 173
ORCHESTRAL MANOEUVRES IN THE DARK

The musician who owned the violin was not a violinist. He was in fact the one who played the timpani or kettle drum, as shown by his strength and powerful forearms.

Page 174
THE LOCKED ROOM MISERY

He fired a stone through the window using a slingshot in the courtyard, shattering the Yuan vase on the mantelpiece and rendering it worthless.

Page 177

THE MOBILE HORDE

He used 11 crates. Seven of them contained eight large boxes, and four of them contained ten small boxes. 7 x 8 = 56, 4 x 10= 40, and 56 + 40 = 96.

Page 178

THE UNRELIABLE DONOR

He simply spoke to Bernard and gave him another 100 francs, with the understanding that if Bernard handed it straight back, he could get a cut of Lupin's 1,000 francs.

Page 180

THE TEMPESTUOUS SCENE

The couple were actors in a play, and the words on the paper were the woman's next lines. The man was a stage hand assigned to pass the paper to her when she forgot her lines.

Page 181

THE FORGED CERTIFICATE

Because they had been looking for the forger of these documents and, realizing they had found him, were relieved and intended to get his details so they could call the police, who Lupin suspected were already on their way . . .

Page 183

THE UNACCEPTABLE MONEY

Because they are United States Dollar bills, as indicated by the use of green ink and cotton. Franc notes tended to use a mix of different shades.

Page 184

THE GREENHOUSE

1) Sweet pea (*Lathyrus odoratus*); 2) Blue morning glory (*Ipomoea indica*); 3) Emerald vine (*Strongylodon macrobotrys*); 4) Golden pothos (*Epipremnum aureum*); 5) Lady Banks' rose (*Rosa banksiae*); 6) Bee orchid (*Ophrys apifera*); 7) Monkey cups (*Nepenthe*).

Page 186

THE PERFECT VICTIM

Because he had no remaining vices for Sir Derringer to blackmail him about.

Page 187

THE GOLDEN TRAP

First, he weighs three bars on one side, three on the other. If the scales are evenly balanced, the remaining bar has the 1 percent lead. If one side leans over, the bar is on that side. Then he weighs two of the three bars from that group. If they are evenly balanced, the excluded bar is the impure one, and if one of the bars on the scale is lighter, the answer is obvious.

Page 188

THE HELMS OF THE RED DEATH

Lupin knows his helm is red. This is because Grognard, from his view at the back, would see the colours of their helms. If Perceval and Lupin wore two black helms, Grognard would know he wore a red helm, but as he didn't know, then Lupin knows at least one of them wears a red helm. Then Lupin knows Perceval did not see him in a black helm, because Perceval heard Grognard's uncertainty and therefore knew that he and Lupin were either wearing two red helms or one black, one red. If Lupin wore a black helm, Perceval would know he wore red, therefore, as Perceval does not know, Lupin must be wearing a red helm.

Page 190

HERLOCK SHOLMES AND THE MONA LISAS

a) Following logic, it must be Alphonse. If Louis is telling the truth, then Alphonse must be lying and therefore Romain would also be telling the truth, which cannot be. If Romain is telling the truth, then Louis' assertion that Alphonse is a liar cannot be true either. Only Alphonse's statement can be logically accurate.

b) Realistically, all three of them are probably lying. But Sholmes already knows the painting that was stolen was already a fake, as Lupin has the true *Mona Lisa* in his possession . . .

Page 193

THE IMPREGNABLE VAULT

The forgetful Mr König accidentally left it unlocked.

Page 194

THE STRANGE DEVICE

12 minutes. Working on its own, the pump will take 144 minutes to pump all 12 litres (12 x 12). Then when you divide 144 by 12, you get 12 again, the amount of time it will take.

Page 195

WHO IS LISERON?

Liseron is Geneviève de Barre, the botanist from page 184. Liseron is a type of weed and she loves plants, speaks of carnivorous plants and lures like the bee orchid, and seems very unobtrusive and harmless but is skilled with science. Furthermore, the first letter of each of the Latin names of her favourite plants spells "LISERON" when put in the correct order: 1) Sweet pea (*Lathyrus odoratus*); 2) Blue morning glory (*Ipomoea indica*); 3) Emerald vine (*Strongylodon macrobotrys*); 4) Golden pothos (*Epipremnum aureum*); 5) Lady Banks' rose (*Rosa banksiae)*; 6) Bee orchid (*Ophrys apifera*); 7) Monkey cups (*Nepenthes*).

Page 196

THE CAPTURE OF LISERON

a) Liseron is dressed as Lupin, disguising her natural voice with croakiness, and wearing a device under her coat pumping gas into the room. The "Liseron" at her feet is an actress, as evidenced by her makeup and dramatic delivery, and then forgetting her lines and having to be prompted.

b) Lupin is the man entering the room wearing Le Troglodiste's old gas mask, protecting him from the gas.

Page 198

THE DEATH OF LUPIN

Of course not! When Lupin grabbed Liseron, her pistol exploded, killing her, but Lupin was protected by Le Troglodiste's suit. Ganimard was still suggestible from the gas, so when Lupin told him he would be "standing over his dead body," that is what Ganimard believed. Lupin escaped soon after, and he has taken the opportunity while you have been reading this book to steal all your most valuable items. *Au revoir!*